HAUNTED WINSTON-SALEM

HAUNTED WINSTON-SALEM

MICHAEL BRICKER

Haunted America

Published by Haunted America
A Division of The History Press
Charleston, SC 29403
www.historypress.net

First published 2015

Manufactured in the United States

ISBN 978.1.62619.585.1

Library of Congress control number: 2015945065

Notice: The information in this book is true and complete to the best of our knowledge. It is offered without guarantee on the part of the author or The History Press. The author and The History Press disclaim all liability in connection with the use of this book.

The dedication of this book is for my wife, Tommie, and daughters, Alexandria, Sophia and Vivian. Without their work and encouragement, this project would not have been accomplished.

CONTENTS

Contents

Acknowledgements

Thank you to the individuals and families who have called old Winston and Salem home. Their histories and stories told on dark, windy and scary nights have been priceless in bringing this haunted history project into existence. I would like to thank posthumously John Levin Brietz and Robert Turner of the Brietz and Turner families. Thank you to Mr. Frank Jones and Mr. Roy Thompson. Their stories and the facts behind them kept the old-timers grounded as they spun their tales of ghosts, haints and the supernatural. I appreciate the use of the facilities of the Forsyth County Public Library and the use of the *Winston-Salem Journal* and *Sentinel* newspaper confirmed much of my facts and superstitions for this haunted project. I also wish to thank Banks Smither and the fine staff at The History Press for providing me the opportunity to present these new stories to the city and beyond.

Maps

The maps arranged in this section are part of a larger "Bird's-Eye View of the Twin Cities, Winston-Salem, NC 1891" map by Ruger & Stoner, courtesy of the Library of Congress:

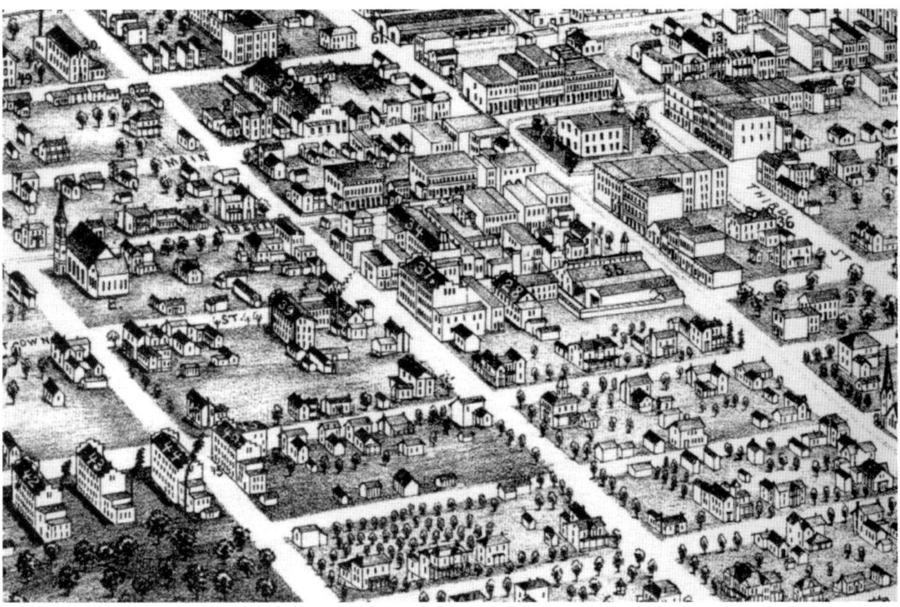

The Central District of Downtown Winston in this section of the Birds-Eye View map includes Main Street, Liberty Street and Trade Street, all at Fourth Street. The number 1 building is the Courthouse at Main and Fourth Streets. The number 32 building is the Browns' warehouse. This map contains the locations mentioned in chapters 10, 12, 13, 19, 23 and 24.

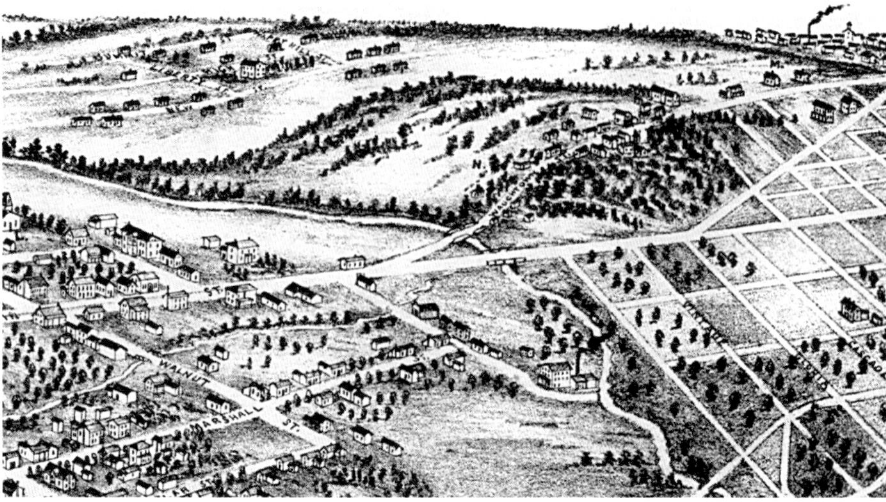

The southern part of Salem and the town of Waughtown are shown in this section of the Birds-Eye map. The road to Waughtown continues in the right upper corner to the town of Waughtown (note the smoke stack). The Salem Mill (note the other smoke stack) is located at the bottom/middle of the photo. The locations in chapters 4, 8, 18, 20 and 24 are contained here.

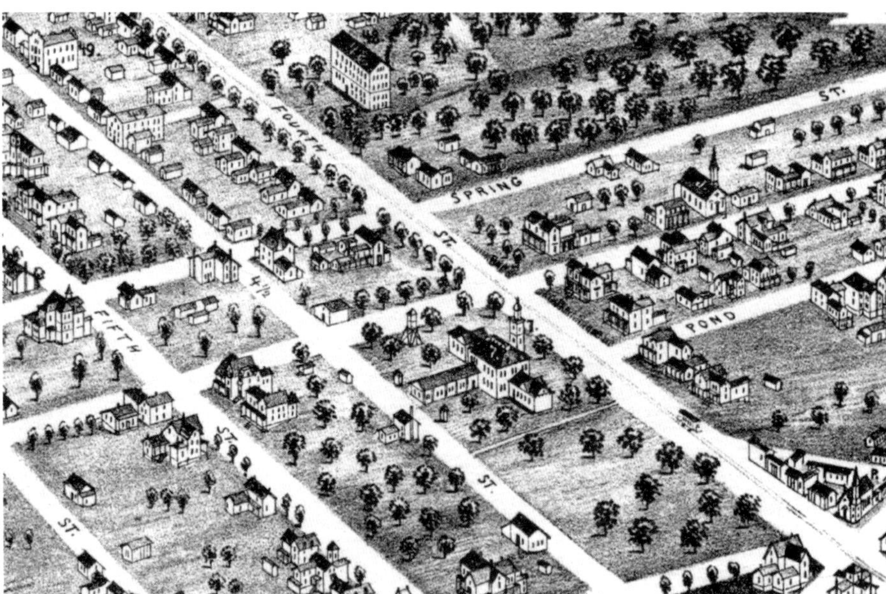

The Winston Graded School number 7 and the first neighborhood of Old West End are visible here. The Broad Street Baptist Church is shown across the street from the Efird mansion. This map section contains the locations mentioned in chapters 14, 19 and 20.

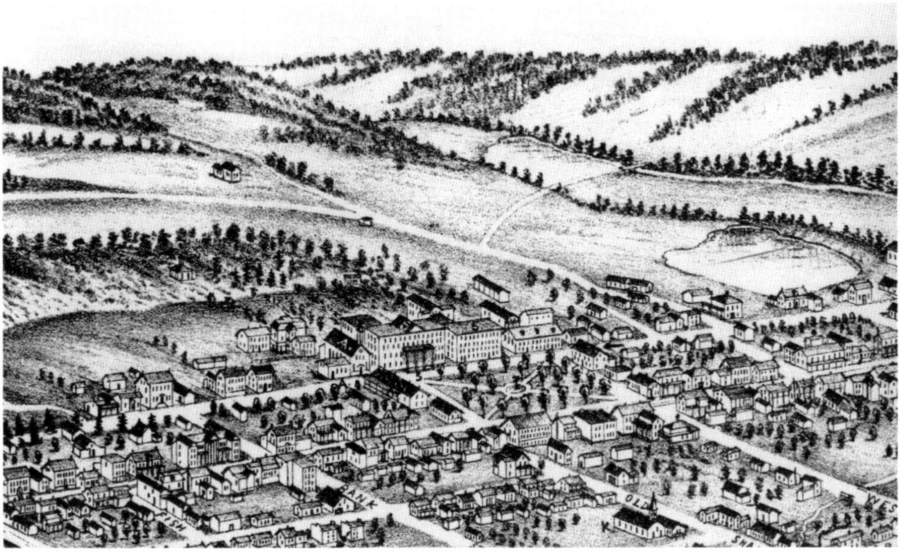

The congregational town of Salem, East Salem, is shown. Home Moravian Church is shown, along with the Central Square. Sidewalks to the upper right of Central Square lead to the Gottlieb Schober homeplace. This section of the map corresponds to chapters 7, 11 and 24.

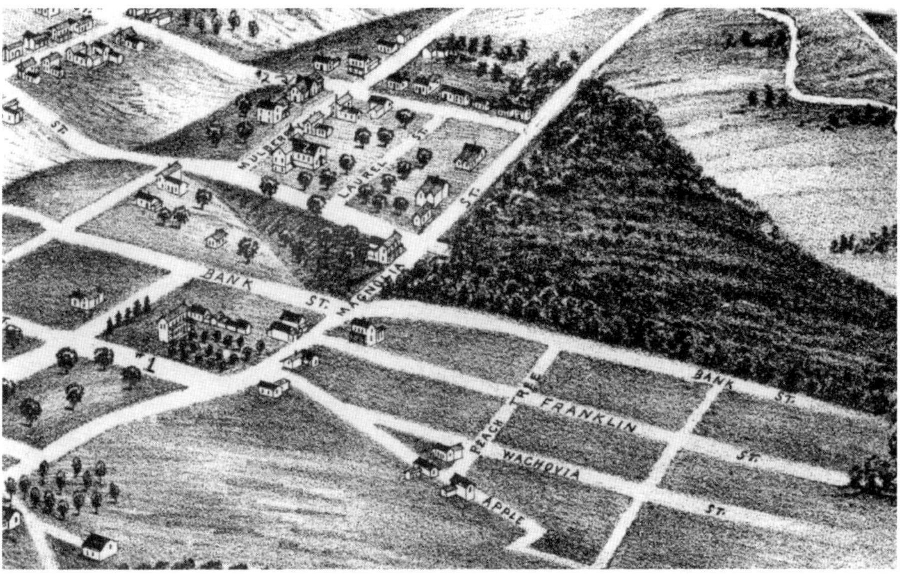

The right of the photo shows Bank Street or Paper Mill Road, the road to the Paper Mill Settlement. The upper left of the photo is the haunted suburb, the 600 block of South Poplar Street. This map section includes places referenced in chapters 1, 2, 3, 5, 6, 8, 14, 15, 17, 18, 20, 21, 22 and 23.

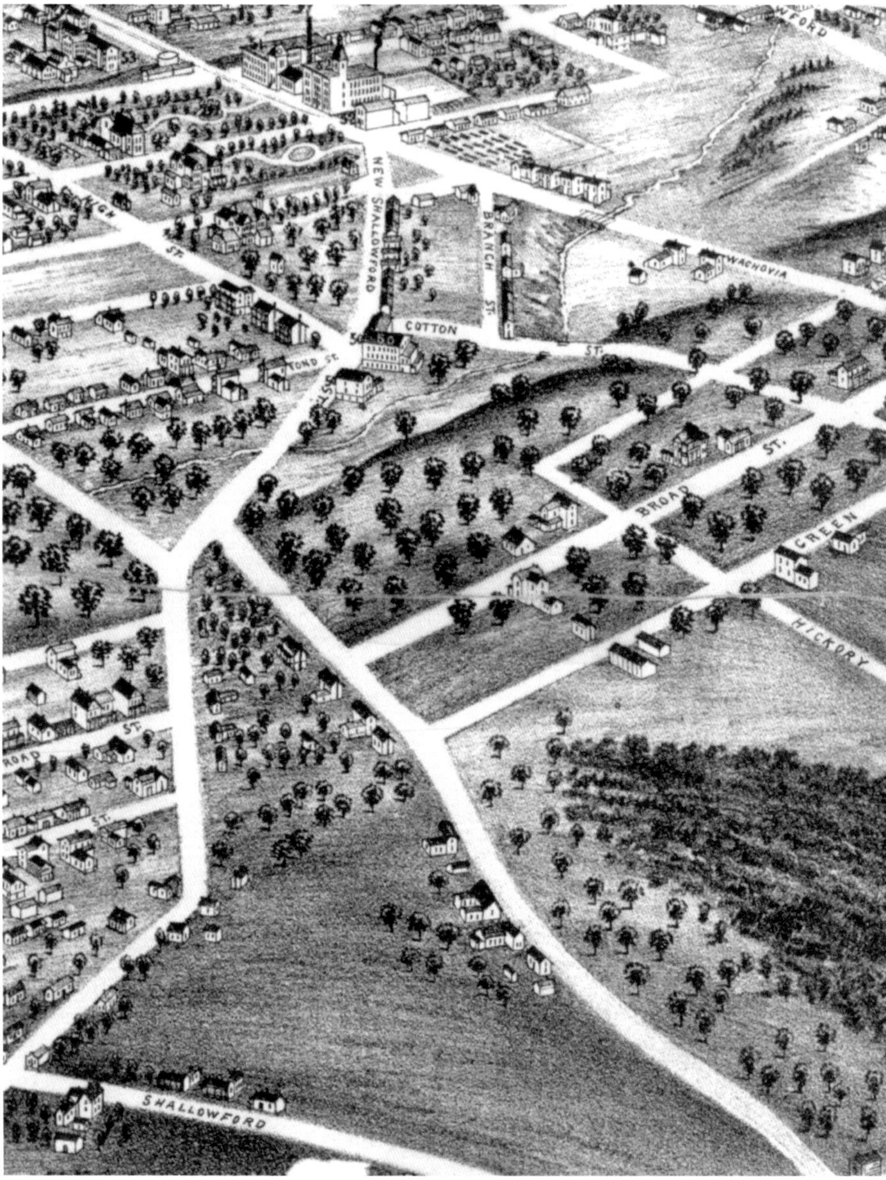

The crossroads, mentioned throughout the book, contained the official dividing line between Salem and Winston. This section of the Birds-Eye View map contains the locations mentioned in chapters 8, 9, 10, 14, 15, 16, 17, 21, 22 and 25.

INTRODUCTION

Why a haunted history book of Winston-Salem, many friends and residents may ask? As a researcher, historian and author with a solid base in local history, I felt a book of this genre had to be written. In Winston-Salem in the late 1950s and early 1960s, my first childhood memories were formed on dark evenings listening to ghost stories told by the old-timers, as the adults called them, in my neighborhood mom-and-pop grocery store, located at the original dividing line between Salem and Winston, North Carolina. The Green Front Cash Store at the corner of South Broad Street, formerly the Old Shallowford Road of colonial days, and West First Street, formerly North Street of the early Moravians, was built in 1926 by John Levin Brietz. Three blocks south, in the 400 block of Broad Street, Mr. Brietz's early Moravian family settled into Old West Salem in 1836, occupying the largest local farm/plantation before the Civil War period. The old-timers who frequented the store often reminisced of Mr. Brietz's tenure as proprietor of the store in the 1920s while conjuring "booger stories" related to them as youngsters in the old establishment, not much different than those told to me as a youngster in the 1950s and 1960s.

By 1958, Mr. and Mrs. Robert Turner were the proprietors of the Green Front Cash Store, having purchased it from Mr. Brietz in the 1930s. At the Turner store between 1958 and 1965, I continued to hear these "whoppers," as the *Winston Salem Journal* newspapermen Frank Jones and Roy Thompson called them. While listening and compiling these supernatural stories and

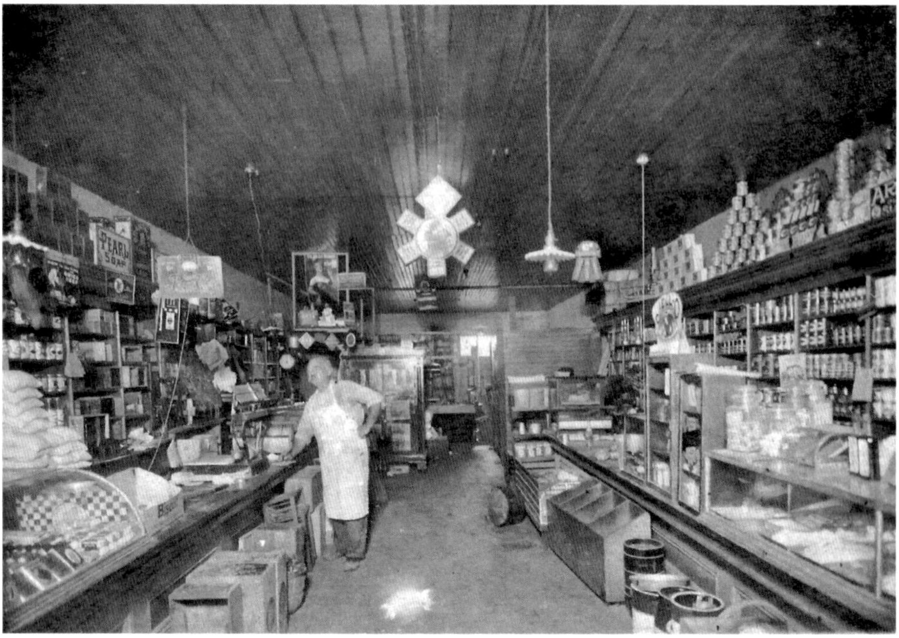

Mr. Brietz, the builder and owner of the Green Front Cash Store circa 1925. This store was where the tales were spun.

events from the old store's patrons in written notes, my hope was to find more historic and concrete evidence of them.

In researching and authoring five books on Winston-Salem and Forsyth County history, I have unearthed strange and unusual stories along the way. By matching my "ghost notes" with the research from my previous books, *Haunted Winston-Salem* was born. Tales of haints, boogers, ghosts and beyond are presented while addressing questions such as these: Were the colonial roads and Indian trails of the Piedmont actually blazed by non-human creatures? Why did Southside's early settlement of Waughtown often frighten the Moravians of early Salem? Did "Old Scratch," the devil, actually come for an alleged wicked lady who lived only a "stone's throw away" from the Green Front Cash Store? Does the apparition of an old tobacco wagon still roll the streets of Winston? These questions and many others will be answered. If truth really is stranger than fiction, our readers should not be disappointed. World-renowned author C.S. Lewis once remarked about his personal search for good and evil. He stated, "There is no neutral ground in the universe; every inch, every split second, is claimed by God and counterclaimed by Satan." So, if that is the case, let us begin our own journey into the unknown.

Chapter 1

The Paper Mill and the Ragman

One of our oldest stories begins with two individuals who, history shows, were as different as night and day. The Moravian records state that one was very successful and the other not so successful. The oldest of the old-timers, Mr. Johns, states this fact much more sinisterly: "My great-great-grandpappy heard they were opposites all right, but more like light is to darkness!"

The first, Brother George Stockburger, was an early arrival to Salem, North Carolina. Salem was the central town circa 1766 of the Southern Moravians. The layout of the town was designed years before the Moravians arrived in North Carolina from their home state of Pennsylvania. The Salem town lot was divided into two distinct properties by the chief land surveyor, Brother Gottlieb Reuter. East Salem, Old Salem in today's landscape, contained the Moravian craftsmen and church hierarchy. The second part, West Salem, was home to the farms and industry. Brother Stockburger managed the largest farm in the town lot located in Old West Salem.

Unfortunately, the records show that the dairy farm failed due to bad luck, bad location and poor management. The Moravian archives referenced many disagreements that the church had personally with Brother Stockburger, which led to his dismissal from the church membership. Old-timer Mr. Johns had recollections of the farm that were more macabre and dark: "I believe the land and anyone who attempted to work it as a farm could never be successful, since many of my older friends and relatives said the bottomland of the farm was cursed." History shows that others tried to

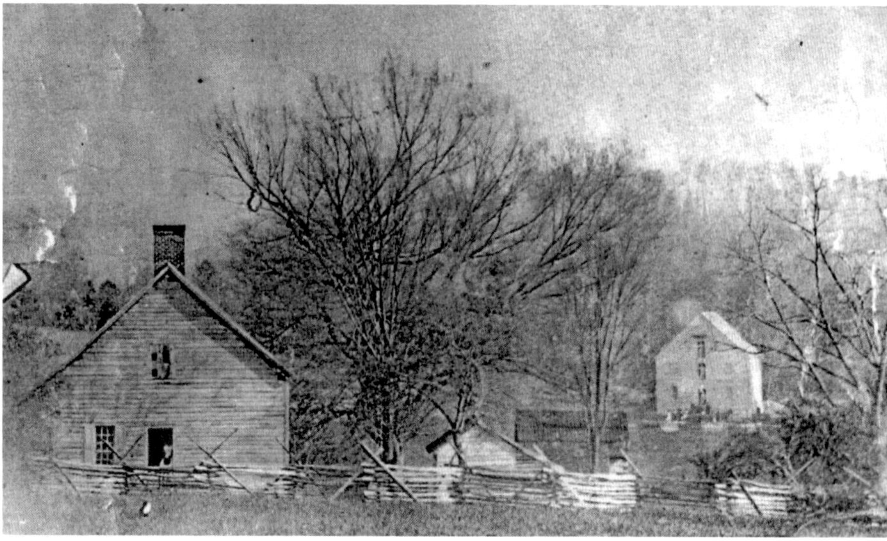

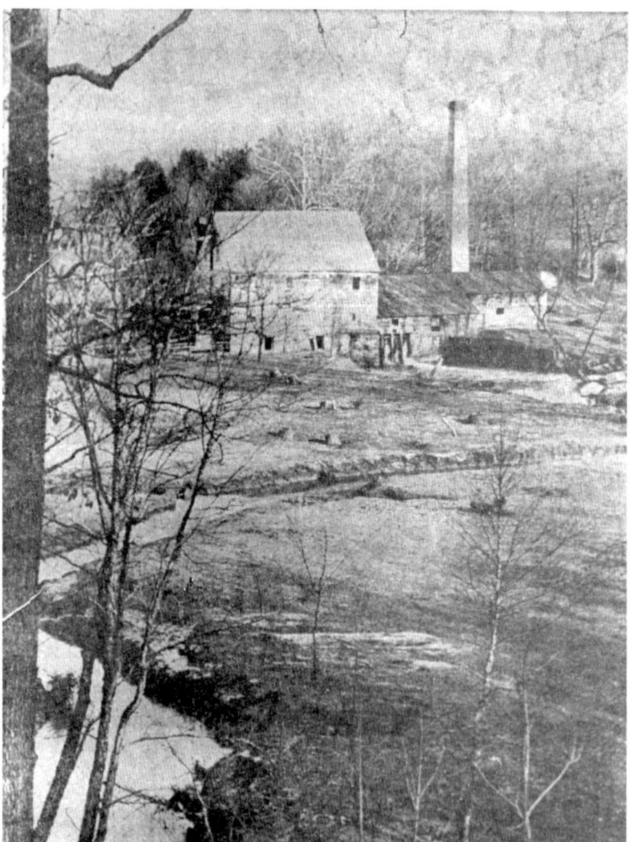

Above: The former Stockburger home site (circa 1782) is shown in the 1850s with the miller house of the Merchants Mill in background.

Left: The West Salem Flour Mill (circa 1820) is shown updated in 1870.

make the farm a profitable venture but were not successful. In 1820, the land was divided, and a new venture for the land was pursued by the Moravians. The Salem Merchant Mill in Old West Salem became the most lucrative commercial flour mill of the town and state.

The darkness experienced by Brother Stockburger was thought to be behind him, but it did not actually pass until a new Moravian brother arrived on the scene. The second individual to our story, the light, was Brother Gottlieb Schober. Research shows that he brought a progressive nature to the table of the Moravian Church like no other individual before him and, some have said, like no other since. Brother Schober (1756–1838) led both East and West Salem through his understanding of Moravian culture, religion and new United States politics. Ironically, Brother Schober may have been similar to Brother Stockburger in that both continually pushed the Moravians' tolerance to the limit. However, Brother Schober's fate as a church member was different than that of Stockburger and much more rewarding. He championed many causes for the Moravians in church and political circles through his self-styled law practice. He served on the Board

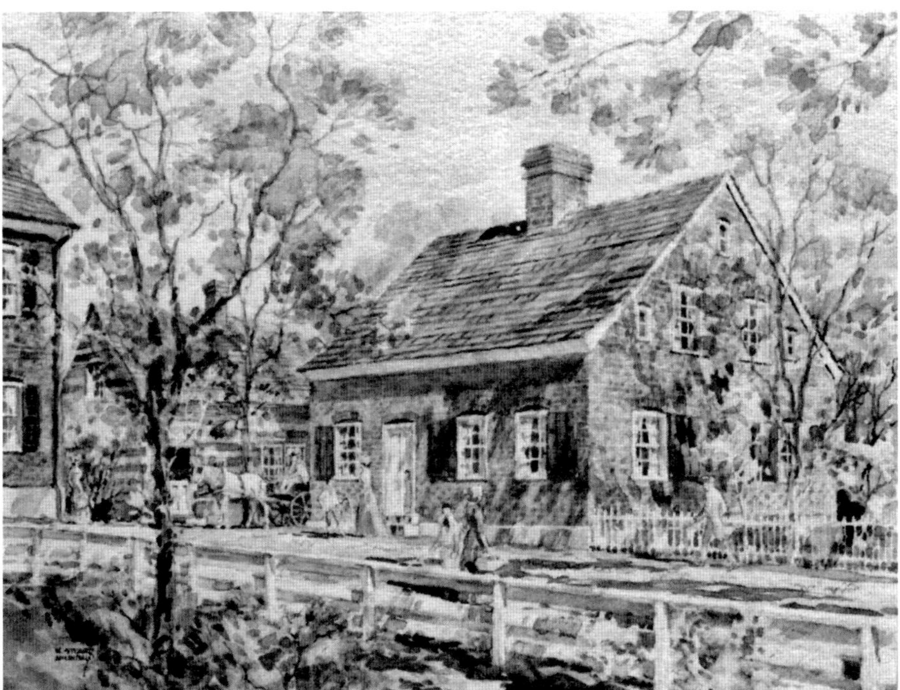

The Gottlieb Schober house at Church and West Streets. Schober was the first patriarch of Old West Salem.

of Elders and as a representative in the United States Congress. He was a true early progressive in his belief of equality for all men.

On the homefront of the Salem town lot, Gottlieb Schober believed free enterprise in business—not the unsuccessful monopolized business practices of the craftsmen—was the key to bringing all men and Salem itself to the prosperity that he saw on the horizon for the nineteenth century. He founded the first modern paper mill in North Carolina and the South. The Paper Mill Settlement of West Salem led by Brother Schober and his family brought together not only fellow Moravians but also Englishmen, Scot-Irish, Quakers, Methodists and Baptists.

Using his influence and progressive nature, the paper mill was allowed to be run for many years in the late eighteenth and early nineteenth centuries by an African American supervisor, a practice that was unheard of in the South and North in the new United States of America. The backgrounds of two opposite individuals, Brother Schober and Brother Stockburger, collided and had a turn of faith one dark night at the old paper mill, which led to a change in both men, according to Mr. Johns:

> *My great-great-grandpappy said an older relative was employed in the Paper Mill Settlement when a haggard, pitiful creature of a man crawled out of the Petersbach, Peter's Creek in today's landscape, to a cabin near the mill. The mill hand, not knowing what to do, carried the man in a cart to the mill. He was helped by the foreman, and Brother Schober was called the next morning. Arriving early to the paper mill, Brother Schober encountered what was left of Brother Stockburger. Brother Schober sent immediately for the doctor in Salem. The time period shows this may have been Dr. Vierling, the resident doctor of Salem, North Carolina. Brother Schober sat and ministered to Brother Stockburger, believing this could be his last days.*

After two days, Brother Stockburger's condition improved. The fever and ramblings beset by his condition subsided. The tale told to Brother Schober by Brother Stockburger spread throughout the settlement for weeks to come. Brother Stockburger explained that he had lost faith, and the bad luck and experiences of the farm, as well as problems in his personal life of family and friends, had made life intolerable. He reported he had even visited a soothsayer, a conjurer who traded in poultices, charms and love potions in the back woods of the Paper Mill Settlement, with the hope of finding out his future in the town. He was told by the witch, as Mr. Johns called her, that his future looked dim and worthless. This premonition was too much for

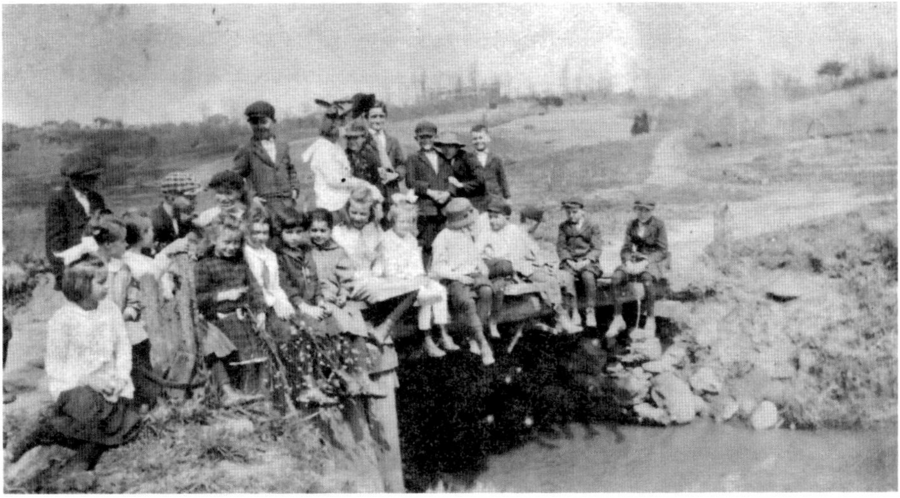

The first class of Granville School is shown circa 1914. The school is at the top of the hill, and left of the bridge (not pictured) is Paper Mill Pond at Peters Creek and Academy Street.

Stockburger, and he ventured to Paper Mill Bridge to end this bleak future forever. History shows that a massive arching bridge built to transverse the Petersbach from the paper mill over the creek to Paper Mill Road (Bank Street in today's landscape) onward to East Salem did exist. Unlike in today's landscape, the Petersbach had been dammed to create the Paper Mill Pond, with a swift current to turn the large wheel of the paper mill. The high bridge and the deep pond would be the last physical thing Stockburger would experience on God's green earth—or so he thought.

The moment he entered the water, he realized the horrible choice he had made, but it was too late. His will was gone, and his breath followed. As Stockburger confided in Brother Schober of this final moment at death's door, he described his last act: a remembered prayer from his youth, spoken as a prayer for forgiveness. Even though darkness had fallen, light in the form of a hand seized his lifeless body from the depths of the pond. He awoke on the banks downstream to find that his will to live had returned, but he had no energy to stand. He crawled over rough terrain until he made it to the only light that shone from a small cabin. The worker who lived in the small cabin near the mill carried Brother Stockburger in a small cart to the paper mill, where he waited for assistance the next morning.

Brother Schober was taken aback by this amazing tale and believed Brother Stockburger had been given a second chance at life and redemption by his Creator. Brother Schober decided at that moment to give Brother

Stockburger a second chance as well. As Brother Schober reached out his hand to Brother Stockburger to seal their future union in faith and business, Brother Stockburger gasped. The light that streamed in through the open window to welcome the new day shone bright on Brother Schober's hand, which matched the one that had appeared supernaturally that dark night in the water.

Brother Schober continued to run the paper mill for years to come, and his son did the same in years to follow. Brother Stockburger became the ragman of the mill, not the most dignified job but one of the most important. Legend has it that even after Brother Stockburger had passed away, his lone voice could still be heard by the townspeople, hauntingly reciting, "Rags for the paper mill, ladies."

Chapter 2

THE WITCHES OF WEST SALEM

Brother Stockburger, the ragman, had a close call with one of the many occult individuals, such as the soothsayer of the first tale, who called Old West Salem home. He was a lucky one, but other citizens in Salem were not as fortunate. Old-timers Samuel and Will were what the locals called bookends, two old scamps who, if they had lived into the twenty-first century, would have been considered to be always on the same page. Samuel and Will, not related, told the same horror story related to each by their ancestors: the tale of the witches' triangle. The triangle consisted of three women of similar backgrounds and nationalities, all considered to be witches, who attempted to extract a meager living while residing in the backwoods of the Paper Mill Settlement practicing their craft. Mr. Johns, the elder old-timer, heard a similar rendition from his older relatives but believed the three were related and were more gypsy than witch. A quiet, educated old-timer named Jack studied at the University of Chapel Hill with a minor in botany. He referred to the ladies' craft as "old-timey science." He stated, "The old mountain remedies of roots, signs, poultices, etc. were simply the precursor tools of later doctors and scientists."

To find common ground for this supernatural story, permit us to return to local history of the late eighteenth century in Old West Salem. History shows the Paper Mill Settlement existed in the western part of the Salem town lot from 1790 to 1877. President George Washington arrived in Salem in 1791, describing it as an "oasis in the Wilderness." After taking the oath of office as president, he promised to travel to all thirteen colonies—the new United

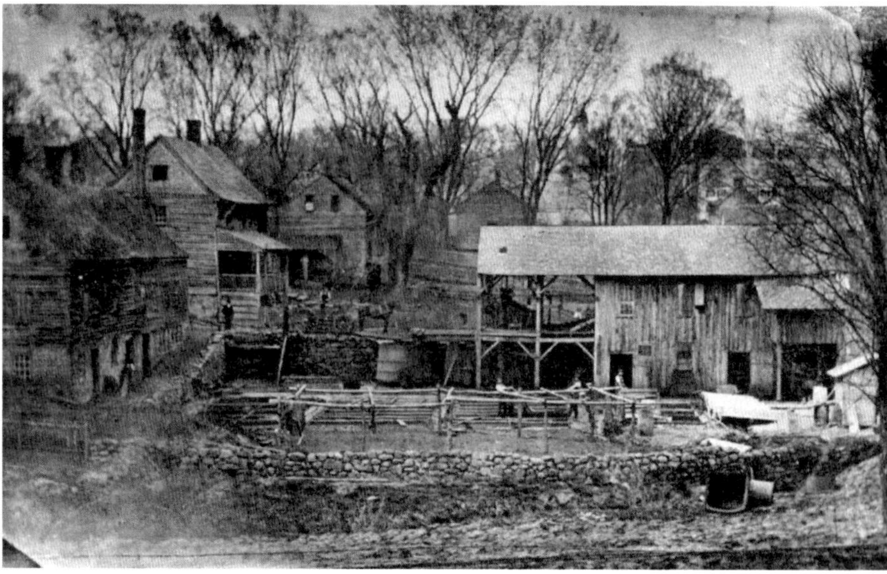

The Red Tannery was the first industrial venture in Old West Salem (circa 1769) and was passed by President George Washington on his fateful visit to the Paper Mill Settlement.

States of America—and his journey brought him to the hamlet of Salem. The president's interest in the advanced water system of the Moravians and their modern paper mill encouraged him and his entourage to stay an extra day in the town. The first day allowed Washington and a Moravian teacher at the Salem's Boy School to cross paths. Old-timers Mr. Johns, Samuel, Will and Jack were all in agreement that the extra day was the beginning of the tale of the witches' triangle.

Gottlieb Schober's paper mill was a mere one year old. The modern Paper Mill Bridge and Paper Mill Pond were under construction. The terrain around the settlement was quite treacherous due to the steepness of the ravines that encircled the area. The president's first day in Salem was spent with entertainment provided by the students at the school. The Moravian teacher, Brother Steiner, met with Washington and offered to be his guide to the newly created Paper Mill Settlement. Steiner had the best knowledge of the land of West Salem due to his many class field trips to study botany across the backwoods. Washington, Steiner and two comrades of the president set out on this momentous second day.

The group traveled west from East Salem on the Old Shallowford Road, the colonial road built circa 1765 from Bethabara to early Salem. Entering Old West Salem, they passed by the Salem Tannery, Salem Slaughter House

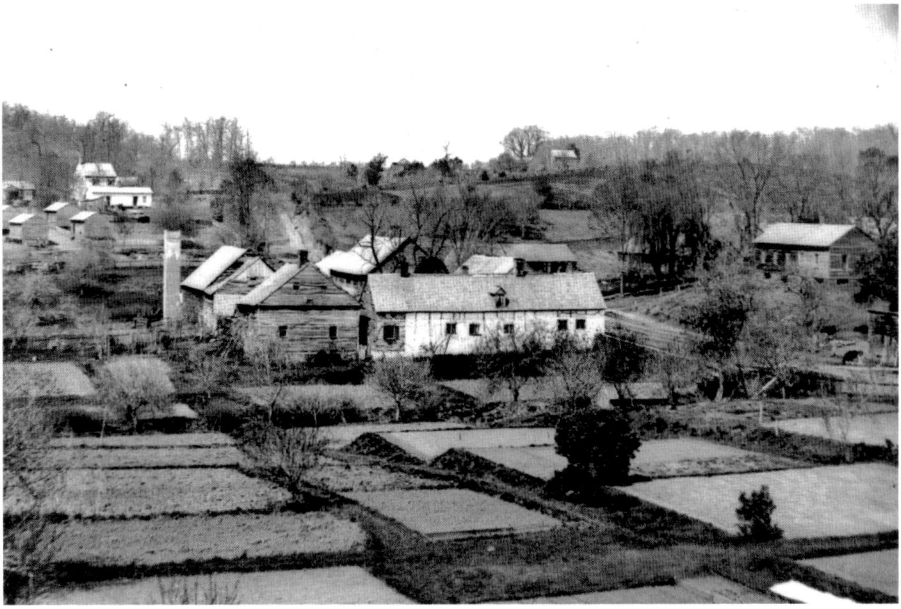

Aerial photo circa 1865 from Single Brothers Gardens of Salem looking toward the industrial area of Old West Salem and the haunted suburb of Salem.

and Salem Brewery, all industries in a few-acre radius. Continuing on the Old Shallowford Road, they arrived at the intersection with Paper Mill Road. The Paper Mill Road was still rather primitive and difficult to navigate in contrast to the well-established Old Shallowford Road. The progression on the Paper Mill Road gave Steiner the opportunity to point out the large farms of the Single Brothers of the Moravian church. This land stretched beyond the town-lot for miles and all was owned by the church. The Lease System, rental of land by all residents, was the law of the Moravians. Outbuildings, cabins and large structures were built by residents as their property; however, if the residents decided to leave the area, they could sell their structures back to the church.

Washington and his men noticed that the teacher appeared rather nervous and distraught as they rode farther west down the steep incline of the road, not far from their destination of the mill. Washington inquired of Steiner if sickness had befallen him. The teacher felt he had to be totally honest, as he was being questioned by the new leader of the whole country. Before embarking on the final leg of their journey, Steiner asked the troop to take a short rest so he could gain his composure. The teacher explained why he was so out of sorts.

It was the land that was unnerving him, and with that, the tale of the witches' triangle unfolded. Mr. Johns related, "Along the steep ridge overlooking the Petersbach [Peters Creek in today's landscape] existed ancient caves and passages, leftovers from an ancient mountain range, which the early Indians of central North Carolina called Uwharrie." The Moravians took their religious beliefs very seriously, and at the same time, they were also very superstitious. Brother Steiner and the church believed that evil, the dark one or Satan existed very strongly in certain areas of the town lot. This was the reason East Salem, the central location of the church and its leadership, was ruled with the utmost strictness of church codes—ultimately for the protection of the central town and its residents. Old West Salem was a more diversified part of the town lot, opened to members and non-members of the church (who were called *autswigs*, meaning outsiders, good and evil). Brother Steiner continued, "In one cave close to our present location live three sisters. Some believe them to be ancient, very old, while others believe them to be young and quite attractive. The church and elders have made this area off limits to any Moravian brothers or sisters." Outsiders and residents of the Paper Mill Settlement still visited the three in hopes of finding fortune, love and health. The tale continues with President Washington asking the distraught teacher if he knew the exact location of the cave. Not being able to say no to any wish of the new country's leader, and allegedly after swallowing a buck load of fear, he replied, "Definitely, yes."

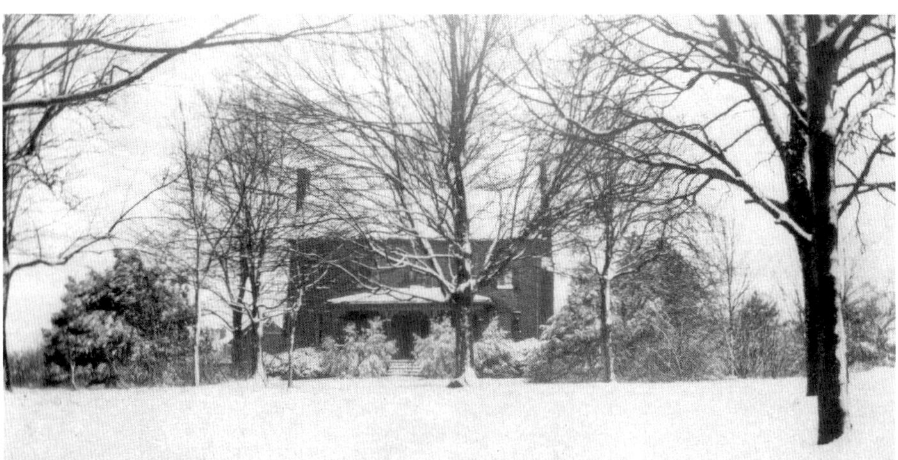

The Krueser/Brietz homesite (circa 1818) is seen in this 1940s photo of the "Monastery," as it was coined by students of Piedmont Bible College.

In today's landscape, most of the cave's systems no longer exist, having been destroyed or covered over by the building of the Peters Creek Parkway project of the 1960s. But at the time of this tale, the cave of the witches was found by the president's entourage. The old-timers telling the tale were in disagreement about who actually ventured into the cave. Mr. Johns said it was the president, but Samuel and Will replied that it was his two companions. They were all in emphatic agreement that it was not Brother Steiner. The process of deduction and reasoning associated with Sir Conan Doyle's famous character Sherlock Holmes can be used here, and it can be deduced that both President Washington and his two comrades entered the cave. From here, the tale states from Mr. Johns's recollection: "Three solemn men exited the cave. President Washington reportedly told Brother Steiner, 'This was not my first encounter with the supernatural or unholy beings. However, I hope this is my last.' With that, the president, his men and the teacher mounted their horses and proceeded on to the Paper Mill Settlement. The tour of the paper mill was successful without any further problems. Legend has it that the details of the cave and all that occurred within would remain a secret between the four individuals involved."

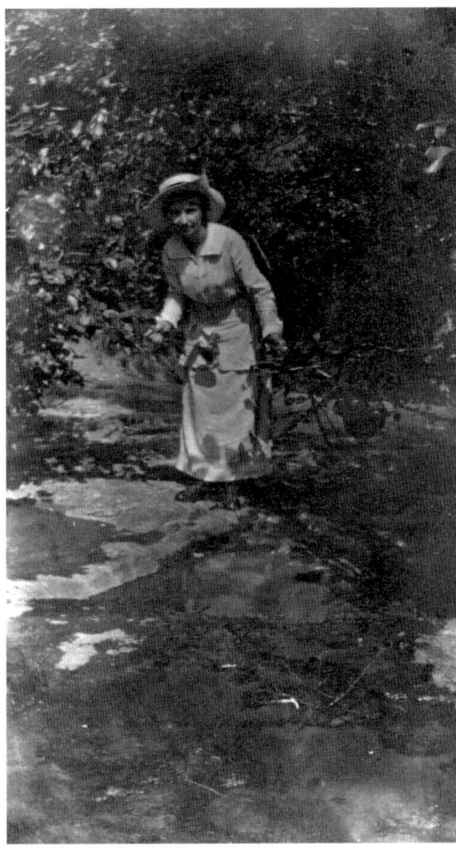

Miriam Brietz is shown near Apple Street Creek, in the vicinity of the Old Rock Quarry, in this circa 1914 photo. This scene was near the Old West Salem caves known as the witches' lair.

The next day, President Washington and his entourage left the town of Salem with great fanfare. The town of peace, Salem, returned to its structural hamlet existence. The Paper Mill Settlement was quite different for weeks to come.

Days after President Washington had left Salem, the cave was visited again by several outsiders who were camping at the Paper Mill

Settlement, and they were told by locals that their fortune could be found by consulting the witches there. However, no person, creature or beast was discovered residing here. The outsiders reported a strange feeling, like one of death, overcoming them. A horrible shock was experienced as they searched the cave for answers to the missing trio. On the floor of the cave lay three small piles of ashes.

After that, the Paper Mill Settlement was besieged with an assortment of illnesses and bad luck. For many weeks, screams were heard throughout the cave system in the dead of night. The local workers of the rock quarry close by reported seeing apparitions of three ghostly ladies traversing the streams that fed the Petersbach.

With time, the Paper Mill Settlement returned to normal, as did the town lot, though over time sightings and experiences of supernatural events and beings would return as well. For this story, I will leave my readers with two unanswered questions. Both questions were on the lips of the old-timers and my own. First, what did President Washington encounter the second day in the sinister cave? Secondly, but even more important, what did he do to the three witches to leave only three piles of ash?

Chapter 3

A Bridge Too Far

Brother Stockburger's suicide attempt was not the only tragedy that occurred around the Paper Mill Bridge of Old West Salem. Mr. Johns reported that drownings occurred in Paper Mill Pond and the Petersbach. The Paper Mill Settlement became a very busy way station for individuals and families between 1805 and 1820. The Great Migration of 1805–1820 began in the settlement after the Salem town lot was designated as a post town by the presidential administration of Thomas Jefferson. Earlier, before President Washington passed away in 1799, he announced Salem, his oasis in the wilderness, was his choice for the post town in the Southeast. The post town project was a federal plan to provide a way station for future settlers of the new United State's Territories beyond the original thirteen states. During this fifteen-year time period, a wagon train of new immigrants arrived in the settlement each week. The parties camped for several days in the settlement of Old West Salem and then ventured to the congregational side of East Salem in order to trade and barter with the Moravian craftsman and store houses. Each week for fifteen years, a diverse class of European settlers followed their dreams to colonize territories west of the thirteen states to the Mississippi River. Mr. Johns compared the settlement to an early version of the twentieth-century Ellis Island of New York City fame. He also compared the settlement to Grand Central Station, except the railroads were preceded by Nissen wagons exiting three distinct roads, leaving the settlement headed northwest, west or southwest. The old-timers said the settlement became one of the busiest one-stop communities in the Southeast from 1805 to 1850.

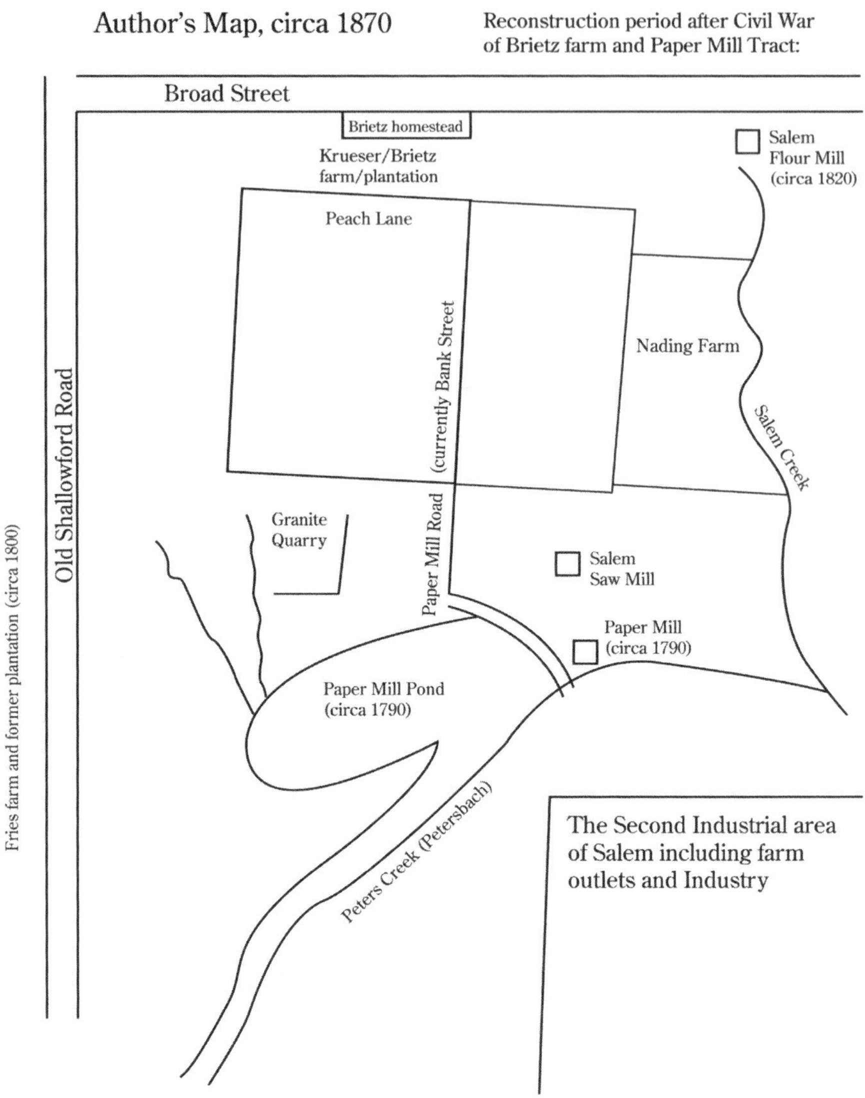

Between 1790 and 1877, the paper mill of Winston was a center of industry and diversity.

Unfortunately, two monumental events were devastating to the Paper Mill Settlement's forty-five-year reign. Before the reign ended, the first gold rush in the country began in the Piedmont region of North Carolina. This first gold rush added extensively to the number of diverse people who, after striking it rich, gathered their belongings, joined up with one of the wagon

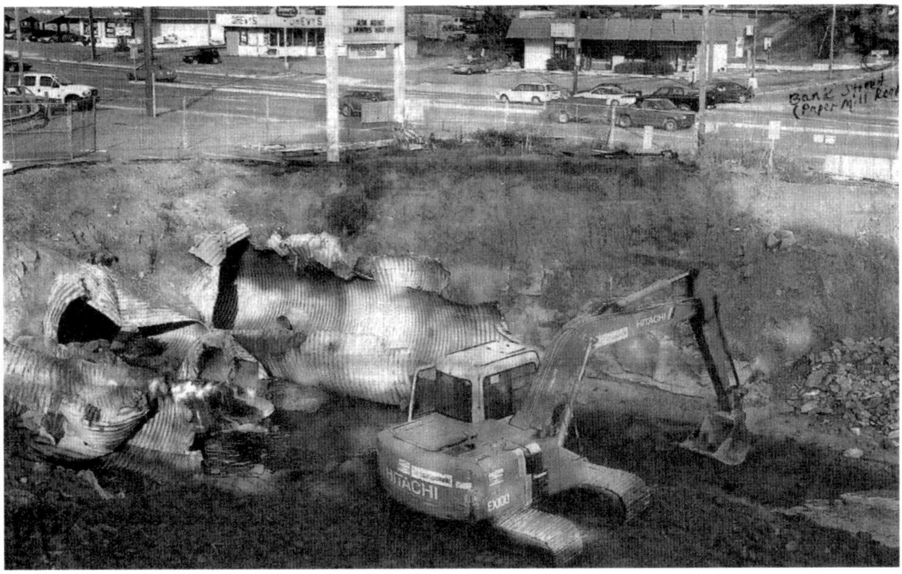

Peters Creek at Bank Street and Academy Street today shows the steepness of the creek to the ridges of the old Paper Mill Settlement and the caves of Old West Salem.

trains and trekked west from one of the three Paper Mill Roads to their own happily ever after. With the advent of the 1840 California gold rush, the Paper Mill Settlement became a less central point since the gold strikes had moved to California from North Carolina.

The second monumental event of the "one-two punch," as the old-timers called it, brought not only a loss of business and prestige to the settlement but also human suffering and death. The devastating event was called the Great Flood of 1850. That year brought the most rainfall the Moravians had seen since settling in the hamlet of Salem. The Moravians were known for their superior craftsmanship in building. Their bridges were built to last the test of time, as the old-timers and many local historians pointed out. The dark time in 1850 is the true beginning of our haunted tale.

The Paper Mill Bridge was an engineering feat, with a massive arc and brick/wooden construction. Mr. Johns, my great-great-grandfather, said, "This bridge would have made even the Romans of ancient history proud." From 1791 to 1850, nearly sixty years, the bridge carried thousands upon thousands of carts, wagons and horseback riders and hundreds of wagon trains in and out of the settlement.

In 1850, however, a proverbial dark cloud covered the settlement, and the ensuing heavy rains of the spring set in, creating a chain reaction of floods

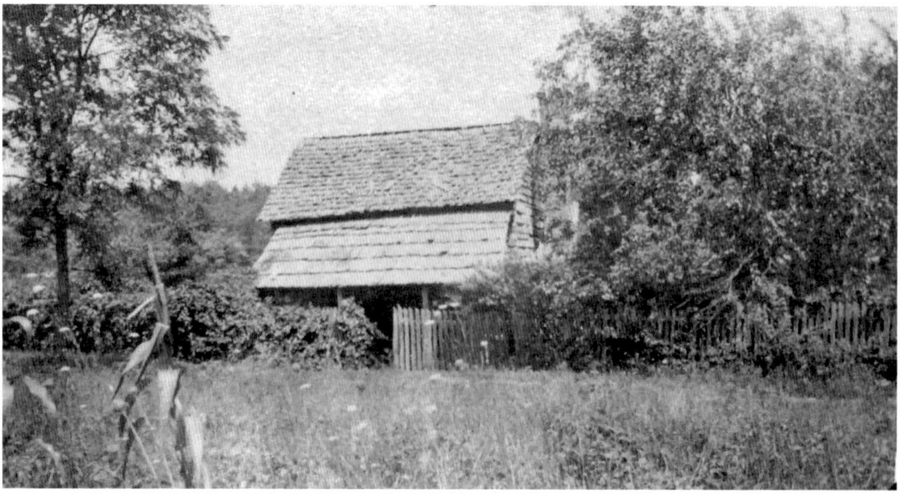

An eighteenth-century outbuilding of the Krueser/Brietz farm and plantation.

covering the Piedmont area. Within several days of this deluge, a colossal rushing river was formed from the expanding pond and creek, washing away all the bridges in the Salem town lot. The Paper Mill Bridge stood its ground. At the time of the deluge, the settlement was still a way station for many of the populace in 1850, but preparations had been made to protect against Mother Nature's wrath. Even with these precautions, several individuals lost their lives, and many more were injured. Even a bridge that would have made the Romans proud could not last forever.

The tale of the bridge's last hour was simply heart-rending. The old-timers related that several of their ancestors were at the settlement on this dark day. However, they were safely on higher ground above the caves of Old West Salem. The sight of this event was frightening and consuming to their very souls. The old-timers said it appeared that the bridge was the only structure of any type that was above water at the settlement. The last of a small wagon train was crossing the bridge, headed to higher ground, when the ground collapsed on both sides of the bridge. The three wagons that had already crossed the bridge were washed away immediately, but the lone wagon on the bridge and the family aboard were stranded. The onlookers from the ridge could only gasp in horror as the three wagons broke apart and disappeared under the raging waves of the torrents of water. The screams of the women and children were heartbreaking.

Attention to the event was short-lived because of what was to come next. Everyone who witnessed this event of the flood agreed with Mr. Johns, who said, "We prepared for the doom of the lone wagon." However, what transpired next, the onlookers could have never guessed. "There must have been some magic left over from the paper mill owner and the ragman of years past," reminisced by Mr. Johns. "As my great-great-grandfather and the others looked on with the dreadful anticipation of the collapse of the arching bridge, a bright, luminescent and somewhat calming light appeared beneath the base of the bridge. The bridge did not succumb to the raging water that battered at its hull. The structure floated as if on a pillow of air, carrying its cargo downriver, beaching the bridge and its inhabitants more than one hundred yards downstream." Once the wagon and owners were safely on solid ground and away from danger, an earsplitting pop and crash was heard, taking everyone by surprise. Then the bridge splintered and was gone instantly.

The businesses of the paper mill, the rock quarry and the sawmill would survive another twenty-seven years. However, the heyday of the Paper Mill Settlement was officially over. Ironically, 1850 marked the end of the settlement heyday and the end of the Moravians recordings of their records in German. English was spoken more often in the village of Salem, and a new, simpler type of bridge construction had replaced a bridge that was built to stand the test of time.

Chapter 4

THE BOOGER COMES AT NIGHT

In our previous tales, we have touched on supernatural events and witchcraft. The fourth installment concerns a monster or man. The ancient Native Americans believed it to be something of both. The bigfoot/sasquatch legend has been around forever. The early Saponi and Cherokee Indian tribes of the Piedmont, dating back eight thousand years, speak of these creatures throughout their history. The respect that the Indians show all creatures and their lands may have led to the legendary encounters with an ancient race of sasquatch roaming the lower region of the ancient Uwharrie Mountains. The Native Americans created the trails used later by the English, French and Scots-Irish settlers to the Piedmont. The settlers built roads over these Indian trails, and these roads evolved into the modern road systems of today. In an even earlier time, the Indian tribes followed the now extinct ancient hairy buffalo herds as they cut paths through the pristine environment of the Piedmont. These paths became the Indian trails. By local Indian legends, the Native Americans were not the only two-legged creatures to follow these same trails. Often, bands of traveling Indians crossed paths with these other two-legged creatures in the wilds of the Piedmont.

The sasquatch beings were said by Indian legend to have walked alongside Native Americans, with the Indians on one side of the path and the creatures on the other. The young children of the tribe tracked with their parents on their first hunting expeditions. The children's naïve description of what they encountered was vivid and downright frightening when related by the old-timers. As a young person myself hearing these stories, I automatically

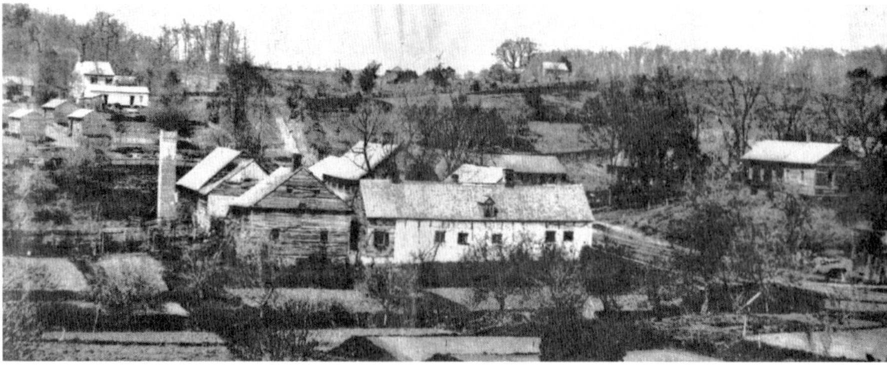

Old West Salem industrial area with the haunted suburb above.

sensed a connection with the young Indians and proceeded to blurt out a succession of questions that took the old-timers by surprise, since I was more a listener than a talker. The old-timers' nickname for me was "the quiet one," but that was not the case this evening.

I rattled off these questions, which the old-timers were then happy to answer. What did the young Indians see? How did they react to what they encountered? What did the creatures look like? Jack, the college-educated old-timer, answered these questions and many more.

The "more" was in the form of background history of the area of the Indian party and the sasquatch. Jack had ancestors who resided in Baggetown, a small hamlet a few miles southeast of Salem. Brother Taggort Bagge, one of the earliest Moravians to settle Salem, had developed land and business for the Moravians, and the town was named for him. As the hamlet of Baggetown grew, the large and successful Nissen Wagon Works, whose wagons traversed the western territories of the future states of the country, located here.

A new individual arrived to town in the mid-eighteenth century. His name was James Waugh. He would make the town his own, and with that, a name change occurred as Baggetown became Waughtown. Waughtown still exists as one of Winston-Salem's oldest neighborhoods. As Waughtown grew as a town, many residents of Salem and Winston moved to the south and east of the town. Along with Waughtown, the other late nineteenth-century neighborhoods of Southside and Sunnyside were developed.

Baggetown and then, circa 1800, Waughtown contained many of the eastern roads in and out of Salem for more than one hundred years. Paths crossed between residents of Salem and Waughtown and the beasts called sasquatch on numerous occasions throughout history. Jack explained, "My early ancestors were trappers and traded with the early Saponi and Cherokee. Our first tale of the Sasquatch encounter related by an Indian elder to my kin transpired on an Indian trail in the outskirts of the future, less than five miles southeast of Salem. The tribal hunting party with youths in accompaniment was tracking game in the early eighteenth century. Their paths suddenly crossed with the wooly buffalo, a nearly extinct breed, smaller than the buffalo of western notoriety; however, this journey was different. As the Native Americans approached a turn in the path, what at first appeared to be one of the hairy buffalo gave the lead Indian and the little ones an eye-opening experience. Headed in the Indians' direction was not one but an enclave of sasquatch. The family of bigfoot included a male leader about eight feet tall, a female about seven feet tall and four smaller ones measuring between six and four feet tall. What surprised the Indian youths was that the Sasquatch family literally moved to the right of the path while walking in a straight line in descending height. The young Indians immediately were told by the lead Indian to look straight ahead and not focus on the hairy beasts. The youths noticed that as the lead Indian passed the lead bigfoot, a simple nod by the Indian was given. The youths were frozen in fear.

The party of Native Americans tracked nearly a mile before the lead Indian stopped and further explained what everyone had just encountered. He explained that his ancient ancestors had existed alongside these "Holy Ones" for thousands of years. The lead Indian spoke as if he were consumed by "Great Spirit," their Indian god. He related to the hunting party and the rest of the village how the Great Spirit had created the hairy beast to watch over their people and protect them in their earthly journey. Mr. Johns related a profound statement from the lead Indian: "All are our brothers,

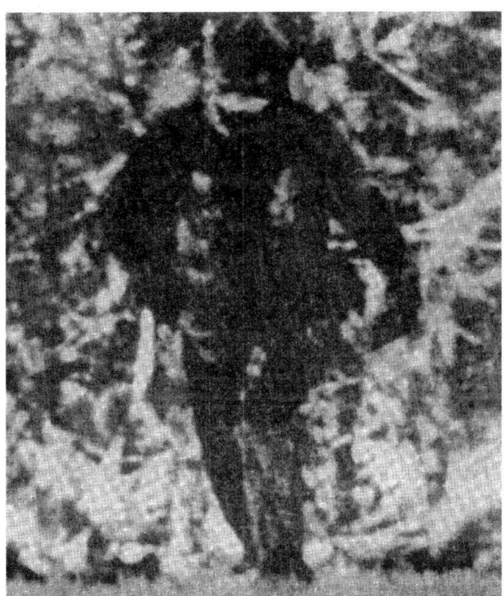

This bigfoot photo is circa the 1960s.

and if any future encounters with the Holy Ones are experienced, the protocol should be followed. No exception."

Old-timer Jack further explained how his early ancestor, a trapper, had an encounter of his own while tracking a rare wooly buffalo, which turned out to be a sasquatch. Thankfully, the trapper realized its true identity before maiming or evening killing this Holy One. Indian folklore states that if you harm this beast, you and your tribe will be cursed.

The Moravians of Salem were very religious and superstitious and believed the folklore of the Native Americans paralleled with their Holy Bible concerning God and curses on humanity. Beyond Waughtown and Southside lies the Moravian town of Korner's Crossroad, known as Kernersville today. Waughtown was no Moravian township, and caution was always on the Moravian lips to traveling residents and strangers who passed through these lands.

Our story of bigfoot updates itself with a personal journey of my own into the unknown in the 1960s and '70s. As a youth in the 1960s, I had a relative living in Southside near the neighborhood of the old Waughtown grammar school of the 1920s, two blocks west of the Nissen Wagon Works from the 1830s. A new development in the area had been created in the 1950s, extending to what the locals call the "Woods of Waughtown." This development was formerly a large farm dating back over many years. What I discovered traversing the Woods of Waughtown with a family friend was a tale much older than the school, the Wagon Works or even the farm.

Mr. Dewberry was a neighbor of my relative in the 1960s. He had been retired a few years prior to 1960 and was a self-proclaimed treasure hunter. Daily, he grabbed his trusty metal detector, a gift of retirement, and headed into the woods. His street, Lewis Street, dead-ended at one entrance to the woods. He had unearthed Indian arrowheads, old colonial coins, bits of pottery and the like. His best treasure, though, was shared with me: a place he called the encampment. This appeared to be a settlement dating to pre-colonial times. It included one log structure and several remains of other structures near a very productive creek with an abundance of clay in its banks. He had found hundreds of Indian arrowheads here, along with shell casings from colonial long rifles. Deeper into the woods he discovered old wooden and rotting pens, which appeared to be used for both small and large animals. One of the reference points to this encampment was called the "big rock," a large exposed granite rock over six feet tall and twice as long. I could have stayed here into the night searching for other clues of the past, but Mr. Dewberry scolded me and said, "Not after dark, or the Booger man will get you."

As we headed back to civilization, probably less than a mile, he weaved a tale of a wild man who had roamed Southside, especially through the woods, going back hundreds of years. He said he spotted him one late afternoon while by himself at the encampment. He was a very tall, large man apparently covered with hair. Mr. Dewberry related, "It spooked me a little, and I headed back home. The next morning, I returned to the encampment, and near the creek at the large rock, I found several large footprints in the clay. The bare footprint was two times the size of my own and twice as wide. I have a ten-and-a-half-inch foot."

Mr. Dewberry became ill, and not long after, he passed away. I spent many Friday and Saturday nights at my family's residence on Lewis Street, and often the "the holler of the wild man" was heard by all, radiating from the Woods of Waughtown.

In the 1970s, the hairy one would strike again on Marble Street, one street south of Lewis Street. A rare Winston-Salem winter storm had dusted the Southside neighborhood overnight. The kids and adults awoke to a blanket of soft snow and large human-like footprints across their backyards, ending at the last house next to the woods. A prank, the adults thought; however, the backyards were lined with five-foot chain-link fences dividing times two between each house. The big foot creature with the twenty-plus-sized foot had to have a gait equal to an eight-foot or larger man. There was no break in its stride at the fences, which were built for protection. It was as if the fences had not existed at all for the bigfoot booger.

The old-timers referenced the Native American legend of the "Holy Ones" to describe the bigfoot as protectors of the land and its people. Who knows when our current land and its people will need a protector, but watch out, it may come as "a booger in the night."

Chapter 5

THE CAVES OF WEST SALEM

The topography of Old West Salem resembles the lay of the land in Moravia, the Moravians' home country in Europe. Hills, valleys, ravines, streams and creeks honeycombed the land of Old West Salem, much like the old country of the European Moravians. Before we move forward into our story, clarity must be given to what originally was Old West Salem. Brother Gottlieb Reuter, the Moravian surveyor, designed and petitioned the 100,000 acres of the Wachovia Tract. The center of the tract was the town lot of Salem, the central town, surrounded by outlying villages of the Moravians. An imaginary line was drawn, north and south, between East Salem, the congregation and craftsmen's headquarters, and West Salem, which included the farms and industry of the town. So what lay east of the dividing line for several miles was considered to be East Salem and vice versa for West Salem.

As the town grew, Old West Salem land was used to create the town of Liberty (circa 1800) and the county seat of Winston (circa 1849) to the north. Years later, with establishment of modern neighborhoods in the late nineteenth century in the United States, Old West Salem land was used to create West End, Sunnyside and Southside (circa 1880s), followed by Ardmore (circa 1910), Granville Park and Wachovia Highlands (circa 1913) and Buena Vista and West Highlands (circa 1920s).

Cave systems existed throughout these areas, old and new, in Old West Salem. Our major set of caves related to this particular tale were found in the lower area of the Paper Mill Settlement between the rock quarry and

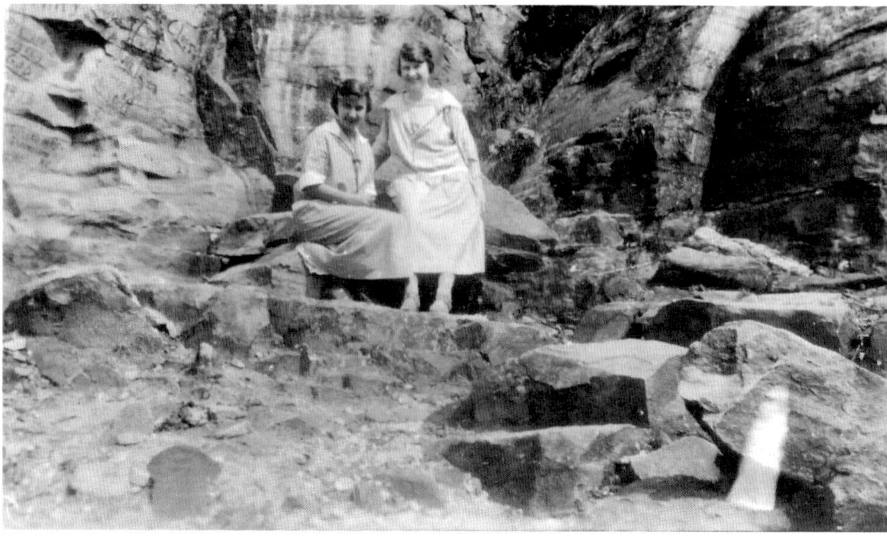

An example of the rock quarry and caves of Old West Salem, circa 1913.

the upper regions of Paper Mill Road. The cave systems were both natural and man-made. An earlier supernatural tale in our book included a cave visit by President George Washington. This particular cave system was part of a natural cave system of the old and ancient Uwharrie Mountains, of which more tales are forthcoming. The man-made caves were just as sinister and filled with their own assortment of haints and boogers.

Our first tale of West Salem caves concerned an early settlement here. Before the Moravians arrived in North Carolina in 1753, a German Lutheran settlement was established less than a mile south of the future Paper Mill Settlement (established circa 1790). This earlier settlement was established between 1720 and 1740. The settlement was made up of a small enclave of German settlers, and they were rather isolated at the time. The group had constructed a primitive fulling mill known as the Langenhour Mill. The Langenhour family members were the prominent settlers of the enclave with their construction of several homes along the banks of the Petersbach located in the present day at Peters Creek Parkway. The houses were located along the creek near the present intersection of Peters Creek Parkway and Link Road. The mill was located where Silas Creek Parkway bridge passes over Salem Creek in today's landscape.

Indian attacks occurred frequently throughout the backwoods of the Piedmont area. The German architecture of the area included rock houses with holes chiseled through to accommodate the barrels of their long rifles.

This particular tale was related by the old-timer Mr. Johns. He states, "The Indians arrived as a small raiding party to this isolated outpost of settlers. The Langenhour settlement had just fought off one of the raids, and the next day, several of the German settlers were tracking along the Petersbach looking for signs of any other Indians. The Indians in the area often followed the creeks throughout the Wachovia Tract since they were usually the location of isolated European settlements at this time-period." Mr. Johns continued, "What the Lutheran Germans found as they searched along the Petersbach in a northwest trek from their homes were no Indians. My great-great-grandpappy called them the 'Little Folk.'" As far as Mr. Johns's relative could discern, the entity was some kind of elf or sprite. Indian legends speak of these creatures in the same framework as the sasquatch.

According to the Indians, an encounter with these beings was believed to be a sign of the "Great Spirit," and respect should be given to these "Holy Ones," because, like the bigfoot, the "Little Ones" were here to protect and watch over mankind. The settlers had a different view of the creatures. The German stock of these settlers, along with the harshness of their isolated existence, bred trackers who were not the least bit swayed or frightened but rather driven in wonderment to catch these magical creatures and find out more about them. As they continued the chase of the "Little Folk," the trail led to the same caves of the future Paper Mill Settlement visited by President Washington in the previous story.

The terrain was harsh and rugged between the Petersbach and the steepness of the cave system that traveled along the tall ridges of Old West Salem. As one drives along the present-day stretch of Peters Creek Parkway from Business Interstate 40 south to the intersection with Link Road, it is hard to fathom what was experienced by these German settlers more than 260 years ago along this five-minute ride of countryside. Mr. Johns states:

> *The small band of Germans caught up with the Little Folk as the creatures were scaling the steep banks of the ravine as they headed for the safety of the caves. Two of the men were preparing to use their long rifles, but what they witnessed literally froze them in their tracks. As if from nowhere, multitudes of Little Folk were seen along the entire ridge. The men later related that hundreds were seen, and like magic, as quickly as they had appeared, they were gone. The men looked at one another as if they were in a dream state, totally dumbfounded. However, reality, if one can call it that, was bestowed on them with the appearance of a giant man or entity as it exited a very large cave along the ridge. The giant radiated an aura of light that calmed*

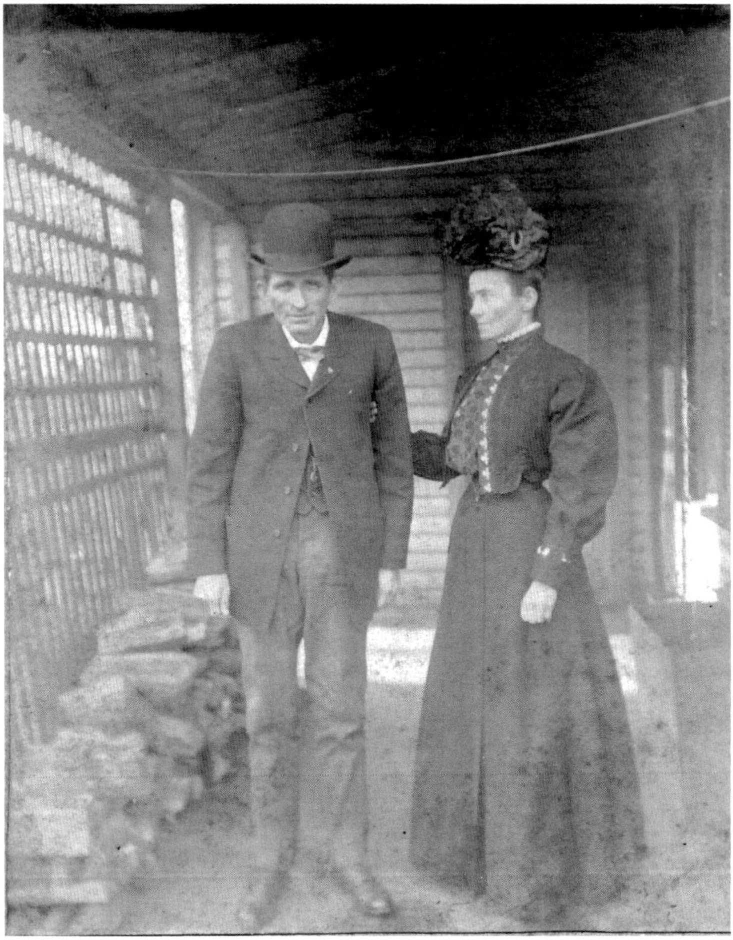

Levin Renatus Brietz and Sophia Blum Brietz on the back porch of their 1818 homesite.

the men and made them lay down their weapons. The giant communicated not with sound but inside the settlers' heads. Later, the men related their experiences to the other Langenhour settlers. The communication delivered by the giant was a knowledge bestowed of the future of their area as a sacred place of spiritual beings, who were preparing the land as a way station for future humans who would spread across the land as the Indians had done thousands of years before them.

With the arrival of the Moravians twenty years later, the Langenhour enclave had kept to themselves as an isolated settlement, never venturing to the north of the future Paper Mill Settlement. The Langenhour settlers existed for a short time with the Moravians and traded at their mill. They sold the mill to the Moravian church and headed west, leaving behind the experiences of the giant and Little Folk forever.

Our next cave tale comes from the man-made caves. The first gold rush in the United States began in the Piedmont. Gold fever spread even to lands of the Wachovia Tract. The Single Brothers, the young craftsmen who were learning a lot and practicing their trades in the congregational town prior to marrying and venturing out on their own, could be found panning for gold in the local streams. Mines for gold, silver, copper and other minerals dotted the landscape and created a mining town period in Old West Salem. Part of Old West Salem land became the sister town of Salem, Winston (circa 1849). Winston was built over old mines that had existed along the creeks and streams in the town lot. In studying the early mines of Winston-Salem before the creek that abounded in the city were culverted, mineral mines in the western landscape were prevalent near all the waterways. In the 1910s and 1920s, a West Salem native and contractor-builder named Charles S. Lee was given the contract to redo and modernize the streets and sidewalks of Old Winston and Old Salem by tobacco magnate R.J. Reynolds Sr. Belgium bricks, cobblestones and hand-made bricks were used for paving in the late nineteenth and early twentieth centuries, having replaced the plank and dirt roads of earlier years. The major obstacle Mr. Lee faced in fulfilling his contract was the lay of the land in the form of steep terrain of hills and valleys in central Winston. This challenge had also been faced two hundred years earlier by the Moravians when they constructed the Paper Mill Road for the Paper Mill Settlement. The Winston road systems were to be built up to even the road systems and ease the traffic obstacles of steep ravines and valleys. Underground Winston was created with Mr. Lee's workmanship. Our next strange tale of Old West Salem caves involves this underground creation.

The story actually began during the Civil War period. The locals of Salem and Winston had to deal with the Confederate money of the times and its uselessness when dealing with commerce in the towns. Silver and gold was always preferred; however, when the Yankees began to arrive, as well as rogue Southern bandits and deserters, a safe haven had to be found for valuables. The caves and old mineshafts became the preferred place to hide valuables. Throughout the towns, these old mineshafts were plentiful. One had to be careful when venturing into these old mines. Many shafts honeycombed under the city, and some were connected to natural cave systems. A person could get lost in them, and the stability

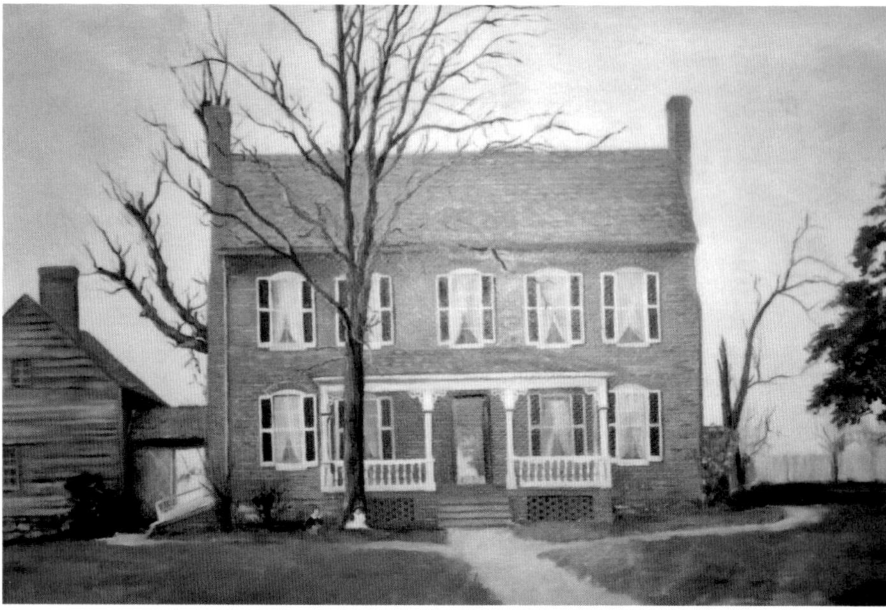

The Krueser house and grounds are the final resting place of supposed haunted treasure from the Civil War period.

of the shafts had been compromised with the floods of 1850, spoken of in an earlier tale.

The old-timers relayed a story told to them by Levine Brietz, the owner of the Green Front Cash Store in the 1920s, concerning his family and the Civil War. The Brietz family had their farm/plantation between the original roads into Salem, Old Shallowford Road (400 block of South Broad Street) and the Paper Mill Road, westward to the cave system of the Paper Mill Settlement. During the war years, the family often hid their valuables in mine shafts they had dug years before on their land and in the ancient caves as well. Many families would hide their silver and gold for extended periods—the Brietzes were no exception. Some valuables were hidden for several years. By the end of the war, the Brietz family had their valuables hidden for such a long time that they forgot the locations of their hiding places. This situation was experienced by other families in Salem and Winston. Mr. Johns related, "Who knows what gold, silver and other precious gems were probably hidden right under their own boot soles—even today."

Throughout the twentieth century, many individuals attempted their own treasure hunts down below the town. Old newspapers in the area have reported that many souls were lost and never heard from again. Mr. Johns

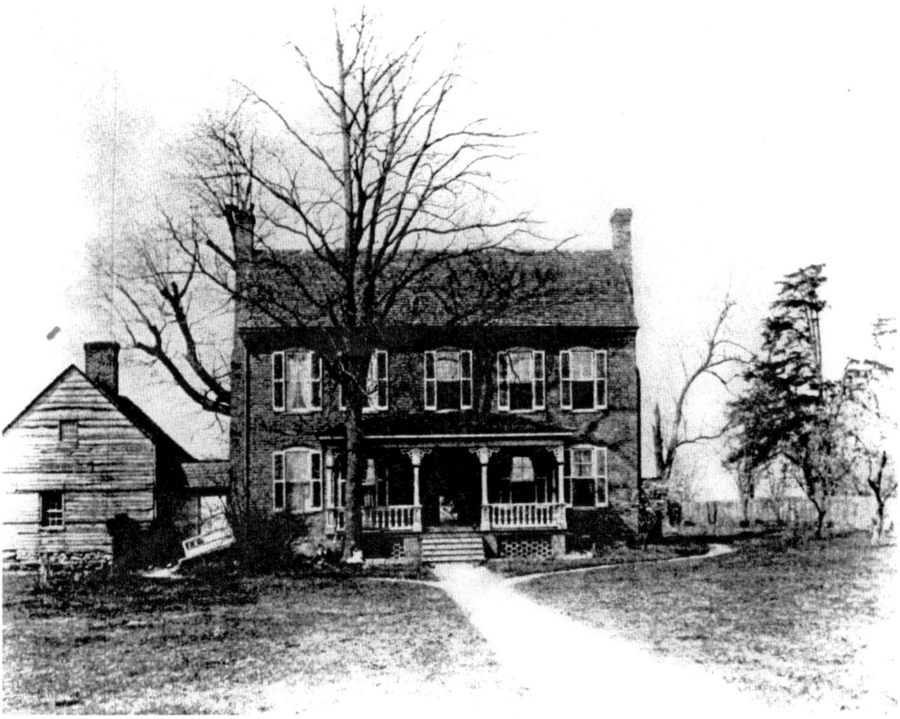

The Kreuser-Brietz homeplace.

recalled, "These lost lives occurred around the many factories of R.J. Reynolds Tobacco. Throughout Old Winston, a factory or warehouse could easily be found, and most were owned by Mr. Reynolds. In the 1940s and 1950s, many of the older factories and warehouses dating to the late nineteenth century had been closed and used only for storage. A relative of mine was part of a group of Reynolds employees who were sent to check the basements and underbellies, as they were called, in these old structures. Their task was to clean and salvage the area and at the same time secure the premises."

The tale spun by the relative of Mr. Johns was dark and goes like this. As they ventured into one of the oldest in the Patterson Avenue at East Fourth and East Fifth Streets facilities, the humidity and stagnant water smell was prevalent in the bowels of the building. The men knew one of many creeks flowed underground these buildings and did not think much about it. They found some barrels to salvage. As they moved these very old hogshead barrels, containers used to haul and store tobacco, next to the base wall of the factory, the men discovered that the wall behind the stack of barrels contained large, thick wooden doors. These exceptionally thick doors were over twelve feet high and twice as wide. If these doors were opened together, a large truck could easily drive through them. The band of men decided they had to find out what lay on the other side of the massive doors. The wall was well underground, and it made no sense for the large doors to be there. A huge padlock that had to be more than fifty years old appeared to be their only obstacle. After securing a metal cutter, one of the largest they had, the men continued their quest.

When the doors were opened, much like fancy French doors in expensive homes, the scene before them was even more puzzling. A shaft, the width of a two-lane road, extended into the darkness. The employees returned to their toolbox for more supplies, particularly lighting. With flashlights in hand, the men entered the mysterious shaft, and the smell and sound of the rushing water underneath was somewhat overpowering. The men inspected the immediate area and found the flooring, walls and ceiling constructed with handmade brick. Wooden beams, the size and breadth of which the group had never seen, secured the shaft, the angle of which slanted downward. The party had gone about fifty yards into the shaft when its members realized there were more shafts, smaller ones, that branched off in several directions from the main shaft they had originally entered.

The story became more intense and a chill went up the employees' spines when they realized where they truly were. They had entered an underground mine shaft constructed years or even a century ago. This was not an extension of the old factory as they originally thought, but the factory was built as a connector to it. Why was an old tobacco factory, built around 1900, connected to an abandoned mine shaft that may have existed during the gold rush days of years past? Also, why was the shaft totally covered with handmade brick? As they pondered the answers to these questions, they were interrupted by lights not their own. Lights began to appear beyond the main shaft and into the smaller connector shafts. The men panicked and thought other Reynolds employees or, worse, supervisors had discovered them in an area they were not supposed to be. As they thought of an excuse about why they were in this off-limits area, they realized very abruptly that these were not employees of Reynolds. The entities they encountered made the men freeze in fear. The workers described them as miners, all with miner lights attached to hats on their heads. These miners conversed back and forth with one another as if they were in an emergency situation. They appeared to be covered from head to toe in dirt and mud, and the clothes they wore were as old as the padlock on the large shaft doors. To the horror of the employees, the strange men never acknowledged them but went on about their business, personally searching the mines rather frantically. As the Reynolds employees gained their composure, they realized what they were seeing was not happening now but more like a movie from the past.

This type of residue viewing is commonplace in paranormal situations. History shows there were many mining accidents, such as mine collapses and explosions, throughout the area during the heyday of the Piedmont mining period. Mr. Johns and the old-timers thought the men were experiencing a residue haunting involving a mining rescue party attempting to find victims and survivors from a mining disaster. The attire of the men put the time period of the disaster as the 1830s.

In any case, the Reynolds employees had had enough of the mine and its past. They returned to the factory. The men closed the massive doors, attached a new padlock on the door, replaced the hogshead barrels in their original alignment and, from that day forward, only spoke of the ghostly encounter to close relatives and friends. Years have passed since the tale was weaved. However, with downtown revitalization currently going strong, especially around the old factories and warehouses, who knows what might be discovered. Mine shafts, buried treasure, long-lost miners' bones—who knows what lies in wait beneath the caves of old West Salem and beyond.

Chapter 6

The Shaman

The Webster's New World Dictionary's definition of a shaman is simply "A priest or medicine man, who can control good and evil spirits in a positive or negative way." Our tale concerns a Native American shaman who arrived in Salem by way of the Paper Mill Settlement in the 1830s. The old-timers recalled these medicine men, who passed through the settlement along with conjurers, witches and fortunetellers with the hopes of finding a suitable place to practice their given professions or what some called their religion. Many in town just called them all charlatans. The shaman in our tale proved to be not a charlatan but rather a miracle to a group of individuals who needed his shaman abilities as a matter of life or death for all.

Our shaman's given Indian name was Running Fox, according to Mr. Johns. Running Fox had a Cherokee background, and his art in shamanism was passed down through hundreds of generations. The quote by author Joann Hailsby in her book *Shaman: The Wounded Healer* parallels Running Fox's knowledge of shamanism: "Shamanism originated in the Paleolithic period inevitably link with the animal world of the hunt. The Shaman became metaphysically with untamed creatures, which provided food, clothing and even shelter. The life way of the Shaman is nearly as old as human consciousness itself, predating the earliest recorded civilizations by thousands of years." Running Fox needed all the training from his past to battle the evil he would find controlling and torturing an enclave of African Americans, both slaves and freed men, along with whites on a plantation farm in Old West Salem.

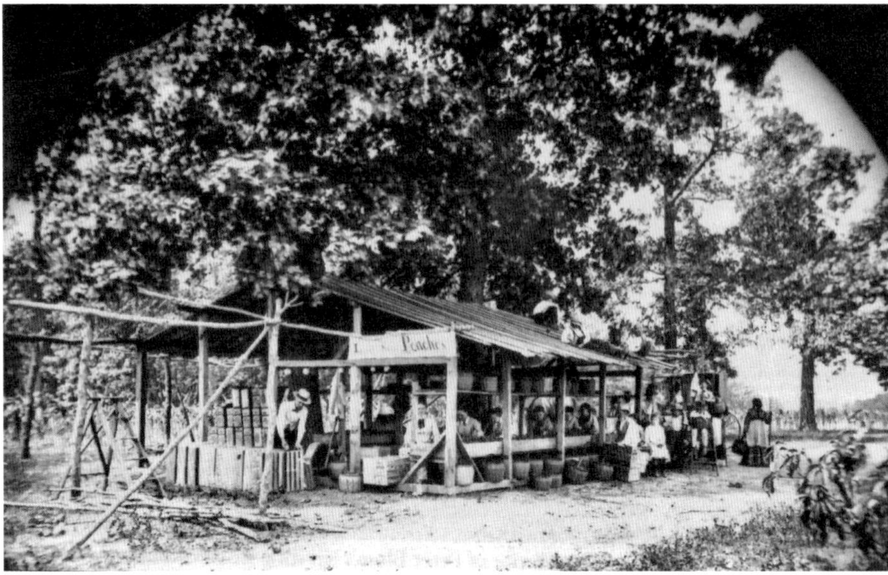

Old Leinbach peach orchard stand on Paper Mill Road at Peach Lane (Bank Street at Green Street, today). Photo circa 1880s.

The Fansler farm had been settled and created from land originally owned Gottlieb Schober, the hero of our first tale, "The Paper Mill Owner and the Ragman." In today's landscape, the plantation land occupies the property of the City County School System, Reynolds High School and its campus and continues westward into the Buena Vista neighborhood bordered by Northwest Boulevard, Stratford Road and Reynolda Road. In the 1830s, the Fansler family could not understand the evil that engulfed them, nor could the Reynolds High campus in the 1920s and the neighborhood streets across Northwest Boulevard to the west. But this evil created horror and suffering for this farm.

An African American graveyard was built on the Fansler farm, roughly a stone's throw west from the present-day Reynolds High School Art and Dance Building fronting Northwest Boulevard. The old-timer Mr. Johns stated:

> *The story began at the Paper Mill Settlement with Running Fox's arrival from his Cherokee village in western North Carolina. When asked by the locals at the Paper Mill Settlement what brought him to this area, his reply was simply, "My vision brought me to this place." With this answer on his lips and perhaps also because of the backwoods buckskin he wore, the populace kept their distance from him. The Indian began to inquire of the*

people of the area what lay due west of the Paper Mill Settlement, as this was where he believed his vision was leading him. Since there was such a diverse cultural mix of people from European and African descent coming through the settlement, it was not long until someone asked Running Fox to explain this vision he was so intense to pursue.

This rendition of the vision was relayed to Mr. Johns by a Cherokee Indian he had met while traveling to western North Carolina near Asheville. It appears what occurred on the Fansler farm made its way back to the Cherokee Nation. Mr. Johns says, "The vision unfolded as a transpersonal realization resulting from a crisis of death and rebirth within Running Fox. The Indian had awakened in a dream web of animal tutors and spirits of the other worlds. These creatures came to Running Fox as emissaries of mythical beings, of gods and ancestors." The vision continued with its ultimate goal as well as its dangers. One has to realize that a shaman's journey, whether undertaken because of a vision or his own accord, is filled with danger. The shaman author Joann Hailsby sums up this journey and vision: "Although the journey is perilous, the ability of the Shaman to be in special and particular relationship with the elements, the creatures of nature, and the spirits from the unseen world, makes the Shaman an invaluable member of his own social condition. This is as much a test for the Shaman as it is for the party he wishes to help. Through the wisdom and work of the Shaman, social and environmental crises can be mitigated and the possibility of survival increased for the Shaman and those he is trying to protect."

As related by Mr. Johns:

Running Fox gathered his belongings and headed northwest along Peter's Bach from the Paper Mill Settlement on foot. He knew the distance was not great and the usual wagon trains, which left the settlement headed across the great vast of the United States, were not needed. He had traveled less than a mile when his intuition came over him, and he knew he was very close to the property of his vision. As he arrived at the Peter's Bach [in the present location of Hanes Park at West End Boulevard], *he viewed a ridge west from the creek and knew this was from his dream that he had experienced, the Fansler farm and plantation. At that moment, a summer's breeze within the apple and peach orchards of the plantation suddenly became more like a late fall breeze. This did not surprise Running Fox, since he had these fall-type breezes during the summer in the western mountains of his village. As he proceeded a few more paces toward the ridge, the Fansler homeplace began to come into view* [located on the present campus of Reynolds High School]. *He realized this was no ordinary wind, and he nearly froze in his tracks with fear. The evil that overcame him at that moment nearly made him have second thoughts and simply turn and run away. Fortunately, his training as a shaman overcame the fear, and he headed straight for the farmhouse.*

On arriving to the location, the fear he was feeling seemed to be experienced by the men, women and children of the plantation. They all appeared as if they were as frightened as jackrabbits, running here, there and everywhere. Once he finally persuaded an individual to stop, the shaman asked to be introduced to the owner of the farm. The man obliged him and took him to see Mr. Fansler. When Mr. Fansler met Running Fox, the first words on his lips were, "What problems have you brought, red man?" The Indian was honest and straightforward, and he explained, "I do not bring problems. I bring answers!" Mr. Fansler looked deep into the Indian's eyes and instinctively knew he was the one who could save his family farm. Mr. Fansler explained how a family had arrived to his plantation during the cold of winter earlier that year. They were traveling through the Paper Mill Settlement with the hopes of going west with the next wagon train headed out. However, the dead of winter and heavy snowfall was upon them, and the western mountains were experiencing no chance of any positive travel weather until spring. The family pleaded with Mr. Fansler to stay and work until the spring when they could be on their way westward. The Fansler family was of good stock and allowed the family to stay. He reported to Running Fox, "It was the worst decision I ever made!" The next morning after the Indian had rested, Mr. Fansler escorted him to the place where Running Fox knew was the center of the family's problem, the Fansler graveyard. Mr. Fansler showed the Indian five graves. The graves contained the remains of the entire Jacob clan.

Mr. Fansler then related to the Indian the following story. The patriarch of the Jacob family had told him a tale that he could not even fathom. The family were German Jews and arrived to Pennsylvania with a Moravian family. The Moravian family offered the Jacob family a chance to have a new life in North Carolina if they traveled to the hamlet of peace, Salem. This was exactly what the Jacobs were looking for, a safe haven. Unfortunately, they found neither. Halfway into their journey to Salem, both families were confronted by an evil band of highwaymen after they had been separated from their wagon train party. The robbers stole their few valuables, but the

Jacob family lost much more. The dark tale became darker as the Moravian family was allowed to leave, while the Jacobs were bound and escorted to the robbers' hideout. The head robber of the gang began to scream and laugh insatiably as if he was insane, frightening even his companions. The devil was said to be in this man's body, according to his comrades. The insane one ranted and raged a curse on the German Jew family. He claimed that the evil one who possessed him was related by the patriarch of the Jacobs family to Mr. Fansler, that the god of the Jews had taken power over his realm in the old country and that he was no longer a king. A language, supposedly the curse, was spoken from the robber's mouth that no one present could understand. Once these words were gone from his breath, the robber collapsed and died. Anarchy followed his demise in the robber hideaway. The other robbers demanded that the Jacob family leave and take their accursed valuables with them. They wanted nothing to do with their former leader or his association with this family.

This incident occurred near the border of Virginia and North Carolina. The Jacob family was fortunate enough to join up with another wagon train along the Great Wagon Road to Salem. They arrived a week later to the Paper Mill Settlement of West Salem. Running Fox asked Mr. Fansler, as they stood over the graves of the Jacob family, whether the curse had died with the Jacobs, but he already knew the answer. Mr. Fansler grimly spoke, "The evil inside the insane man was transferred to the Jacob family, and now, at their deaths, it has been transferred to my farm and all who reside here."

This explained and confirmed the feeling of evil the shaman had experienced upon arrival to the farm. The Indian shaman informed Mr. Fansler that he must prepare for the ritual to rid the farm of the evil entity and its curse forever. In preparation for the battle between good and evil, the Indian created from an old rundown cabin on Fansler land a sweat lodge for the purification of his soul. The quest of vision through holy prayer in the lodge for two days allowed the positive power that guided the universe to guide him on his quest to save the Fansler farm and all that resided on it, including the livestock.

With the accomplishment of this purification ritual, the battle for good over evil commenced. The outcome of this battle was related by Mr. Johns. The Fansler family and all living beings, be they man or beast, were assembled at the evil one's power source, the graveyard. By burying these unfortunate souls, the Jacobs, in the Fansler cemetery, the evil was allowed to spread throughout the farm/plantation. This was the moment in time when the battle began. Everyone present was still and quiet on this cool summer evening, and even the livestock seemed to be struck by silence.

Running Fox began the Dance of the Shaman, a traditional dance that has been practiced since the beginning of our civilization. As he danced, he spoke the words passed down through shamans for centuries. Once these words left his lips, the ground in the graveyard began to shake uncontrollably as if an earthquake was at hand. The shaman spoke in English for all entities to hold their ground and remain silent. A few gravestones collapsed, and the five graves containing the remains of the Jacob clan sank into the ground as if no bodies were ever there. The large hardwoods throughout the farm took on the shapes of hideous creatures as they swayed in the wind. Within minutes of the collapse of the five graves, cries, shrieks and moans rose from the site of the five graves and then silence. Many in attendance spoke years later to their families of the sounds heard coming from beneath the earth as if they were from hell itself. Then the end came. Incredibly, the sounds were gone, the wind was calm, the trees returned to their normal shape and the moon appeared from behind the dark clouds that had loomed over the entire cleansing ritual.

The next day was more beautiful than ever on the plantation farm, and life returned to normal. The same day, the shaman, having accomplished his mission to cleanse the farm, parted company with Mr. Fansler with a simple good-bye and good luck. Mr. Johns and the old-timers never knew what became of Running Fox, the shaman of West Salem. I attended the school built across the block from the graveyard in our story in the late 1960s and early 1970s, Reynolds High School. Old remnants with sunken graves were still in existence there. New development occurred in that block of the old graveyard in the 1990s. It was reported the graveyard was moved with the new development, remains and all, but others have said the land of the graveyard was fenced and is still protected. Hopefully, the land is still protected, and the evil will never return.

Chapter 7

THE GIRL IN THE WINDOW

For this supernatural tale, we move away from Old West Salem to Old East Salem, the congregational town and craftsman headquarters in the National Historic Landmark District of Old Salem. Due north of the center of Old Salem on Church Street and next door to the entrance to Gods Acre, the Moravian graveyard, can be found the former home and business of one of the most prominent doctors of Salem, Brother Vierling. The Vierling home and barn (circa 1801) is currently a museum tour home of Old Salem. Inside this establishment is the re-created family quarters and quarters for practicing medicine in this early nineteenth-century home. The doctor was a pioneer in his given profession, providing early immunizations and rehabilitation of his patients. He fought brilliantly the diseases that plagued early settlers to North Carolina. However, the battles with disease cost him dearly. Death and disease were always at his door.

He lost one of his most important battles when he lost his daughter to disease. His daughter became what I believe to be the inspiration for the girl in the window. My personal encounter with a paranormal event while on an evening jog in the historic village in the 1990s gave me my own taste of a ghost tale. My journey into the unknown of haunted history began one late afternoon as I jogged past the intersection of South Main and East Bank Streets. I was moving from north to south on Main Street and was just passing the antebellum Belo Home. This home has always fascinated my family with its unique history. My children, as well as my wife and I, were

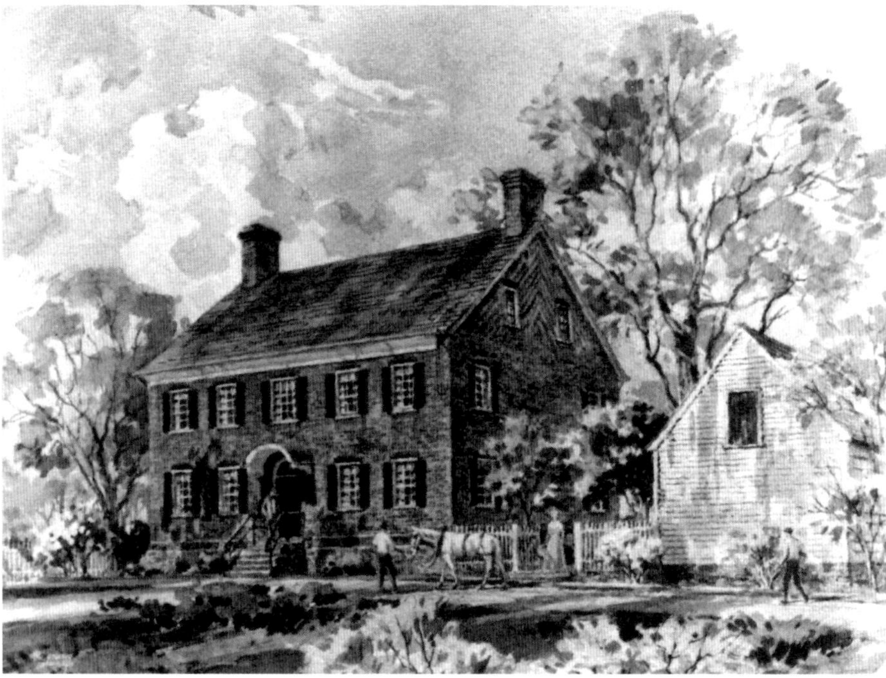

Dr. Vierling's home and barn are pictured in this circa 1802 painting.

taken aback by the iron animal caricatures that line the steps at the southern end of the homeplace. These ironwork creations were advertising agents to showcase Mr. Belo's foundry business dating back more than 150 years.

However, this particular evening had a strange feeling to it. The air was different as I glanced at the shadows up Bank Street hill and against the brick wall of the Vierling house. What I saw made me stop cold in my tracks. In the middle window of the second story of the home, I saw a young girl, twelve to fourteen years of age, dressed in a very decorative white dress of the nineteenth century, I guessed. As I proceeded to walk up the hill of Bank Street toward the house, the girl's gaze appeared to catch mine. Her next movement was a wave of the hand. As is often the case when someone waves, you wave back. So, reflexively, I did. As I drew closer to the house, a realization overcame me: she was not looking or responding to me but beyond. Believing the picture before me of the young girl was merely a residue of a past event, I proceeded to move out of the view of the window to see if she would turn or simply move away. She continued to look straight ahead, not at me, and her facial expression turned from a smile to a grin of sheer enjoyment. Almost immediately, the scene turned from a joyous

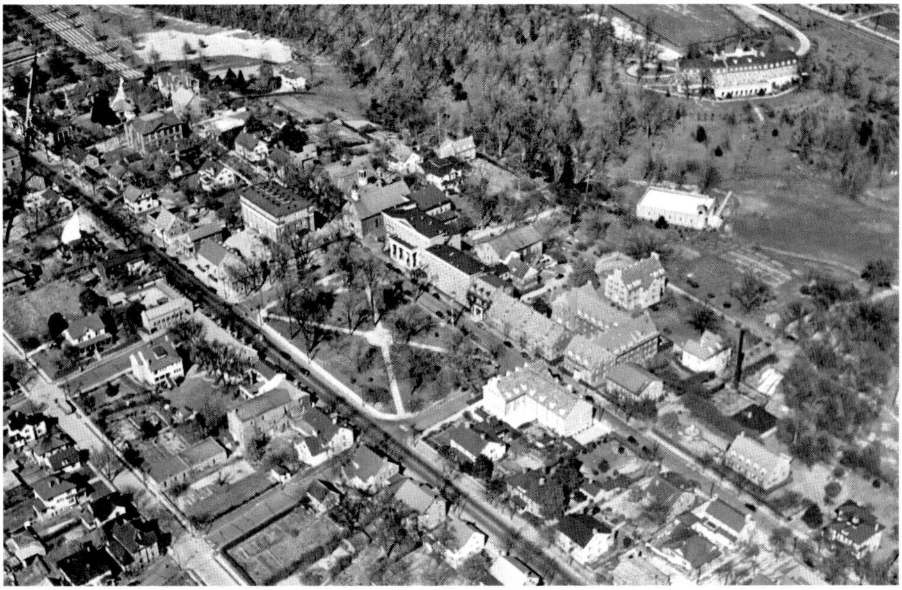

Seen in 2015, the Vierling museum house (upper left corner) and location of the girl in the window.

occasion to one of fear and anguish across the girl's face. She appeared heartbroken and proceeded to fade away.

I stood for several minutes, attempting to process all I had seen in these fleeting moments from the apparition's first appearance. Then I continued my run and said nothing about the experience. The next day, I returned to the Vierling home and related to the visitor guide at the museum home my experience. The guide thought the experience somewhat humorous, but in his voice, there appeared some doubt. He reported experiences he had had late in the day while alone in the old house that were a little creepy. He related that he heard footsteps upstairs, doors opening and closing and shadows appearing out of nowhere, all while in the house alone. He did confirm that Dr. Benjamin Vierling had a daughter around this age when she expired. He also confirmed this was positively not a live person I saw since all the windows in the museum homes were shaded to outside light for protection of the antiques inside. These shades made it almost impossible to see someone inside at the windows as well.

For several years, I wondered who or what the girl was trying to communicate with and visited the site several times thereafter, but re-creating the scene was futile. As I researched for my book *Winston-Salem: A Twin City History* in 2007, I believed I had found the answer. Two events had occurred at the same intersection of Bank and Main Streets where I first saw the young girl in the window. One tragic event occurred in the late nineteenth century. A small boy was sledding on Bank Street Hill, and as his sled crossed Main Street to continue down the other side of Bank Street, he was run over by the streetcar at the intersection and died instantly. Since this accident occurred more than seventy years after the little girl died, even if it had been Dr. Vierling's daughter whom I saw, I do not believe the apparition was responding to the tragic streetcar accident. The second event makes more sense, providing our reader believes in the supernatural and ghosts.

Salem was founded in 1766. The first line of houses built was along the western side of Main Street, across from the future location of the Belo House. The Belo homesite was originally to be the site of the town square and the central part of the congregational town. Because of a water flow problem in the early water system, the square and center of town was moved farther south on Main Street to its present location. My second choice for the girl's appearance in the window was the site of the first two-story house to be built in Salem, circa 1767. It resided at the western corner of Main Street, directly in line with the future Vierling house site. This house served as a hospital during the Revolutionary War, and victims of the war were housed here. Eighteenth-century surgeries were performed at the hospital, accompanied by the screams and moans from primitive surgeries. Could it have been possible that the young girl in the window was responding to the residue action played out to her in the same way her actions had played out to me? The young injured soldiers had experienced the best of times and the worst of times. At the hospital, the tragedy and blessing was seen in a residue haunting could have caught the young girl's fancy or brought heartbreak at the same time.

Another added twist to the story of this notorious block of supernatural action stems from the building that replaced the two-story house in early 1900. The building was a factory and later a mortuary. The story was told of apparitions and the appearance of wounded soldiers that appeared in its basement. My immediate family resided here for a short time after the building had been remodeled as an apartment dwelling. It was my first residence in the world, having been brought here as a baby from the North Carolina Baptist Hospital located in the Ardmore neighborhood. In the closing of this tale, I ask my readers if this supernatural event could have been more a part of my story in connection with the girl in the window than even I knew. Could it be possible the girl in the window had seen more of me over the years than I of her in this haunted experience in East Salem?

Chapter 8

The Spooky Suburb of Salem

East Salem, Old Salem today and Old West Salem have many parallels in their histories, and even more so in their haunted histories. Our previous chapter, "The Girl in the Window," presented a haunted intersection of paranormal activity in Old Salem. Old West Salem deserves equal billing of the supernatural activity in its own spooky suburb.

The 600 block of South Poplar Street in Old West Salem is one of the most unique city blocks in North Carolina, possibly in the complete Southeast United States. The block began in 1850 out of a need to expand the central congregational town of East Salem. The town of Winston had just been created from Old West Salem land in 1849, soon to become the county seat of Forsyth County. The block was the first outside the town to have modern streetlights, gaslights of the time, in 1850. Historians have found that the 600 block of Poplar Street may have been the first modern suburb in North Carolina. The block has been home to farmers, industrialists, political figures, financiers and craftsmen. Another unique feature is the city block has ten structures that span eight decades of history—1840, 1850, 1860, 1870, 1880, 1890, 1900, 1910—all in the 600 block. This small area created an interaction between individuals, businesses and commerce; the positive and negative energy created and fueled much paranormal activity.

Before we begin our ghost tales, permit me to introduce one family dating back several generations who were single-handedly responsible for keeping the block intact for more than one hundred years. The Ruff family descended from German and Moravian stock. Their effort, begun by John

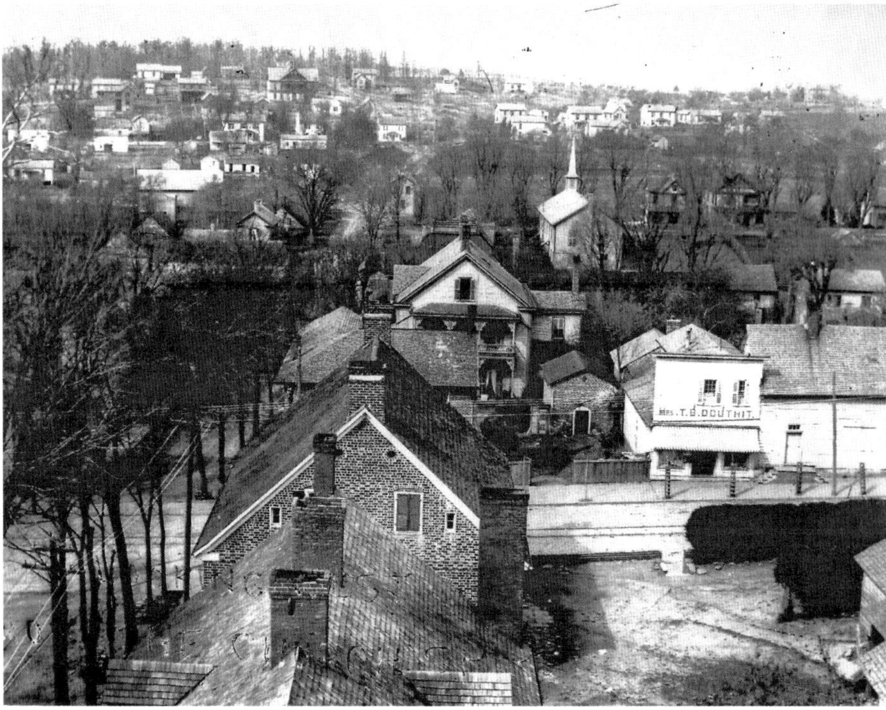

This circa late 1890s aerial photo from the steeple of Home Moravian Church in Salem shows Old Salem and Old West Salem with West Salem Graded School (circa 1895) and the haunted suburb clearly.

Ruff Sr., preserved the historical character of the block long before historical preservation of towns and cities across America were even imagined. Their history and preservation allowed the Old West Salem Historic District to have the momentum to come into existence. The Preserve America Neighborhood distinction, which Old West Salem has received, one of only nineteen neighborhoods in the United States to do so, owes much of its success to the history of the 600 block of Poplar Street. The ghosts of this block of homes and businesses were experienced not by the old-timers in past tales but by the generations of the Ruff clan.

Our tale begins with the founding of the first suburb of Salem in 1850. An excerpt from the *Peoples Press*, the newspaper of Salem, sets the stage for the atmosphere surrounding the town in 1850:

> *Our village: For the gratification of our distant readers, may we be permitted to say, that a considerable change has come over the spirit of the dream of*

quiet Salem and its vicinity, within the last few years. A new impulse has been given to business generally, and improvement, in various ways, is still the "the order of the day"! Our new suburb is complete and holds much promise for future expansion. Our merchants are doing a large business; our merchants are honest; industry is striving; the bank fully sustained its business character; the cotton and wool factories are in full tide of successful operation; the hotels are at all times prepared to entertain with the best marked offence! And last, though not least. The Salem Female Academy is in a very flourishing condition, and bound to stand, in all time to come, upon an unshakeable foundation.

The town of Winston was still called Salem until 1851, when the town received its name and first courthouse, but for now, the new kid on the block was our spooky suburb of Salem.

The 1850 Ackerman/Reich/Ruff homeplace at 608 South Poplar Street, the oldest on the 600 block, is the location of our first tale. John Ackerman built the home. However, the haunting is associated with the second owner, the Reich family. Mr. Reich was a second-generation shoemaker. His family's former homesite lies at the end of South Church Street at Race Street in Old Salem. A small display marker shows the home with the hopes of reconstruction in the future. Mr. Reich's father was a direct descendant of the first founders of colonial Salem, circa 1760s. The son purchased the home on Poplar Street from Mr. Ackerman in 1870. He practiced his craft of shoemaking and repair and, in the 1880s, built a small brick outbuilding in the rear of his homeplace to expand his business. In the early twentieth century, John Ruff Sr. purchased the homeplace. His granddaughter Bobbie Ruff created an addition to the brick outbuilding, the former shoemaker shop, and began a frame shop. She designed violins there as well.

The connections of the crafts of the Reichs and Ruffs may have been the catalyst to fuel what came next. Bobbie Ruff and her sister, Marilyn, who owned a business next door, often heard tapping radiating from the small craft shop. At the time, they did not know the history of the outbuilding and thought nothing about it. However, as the *tap, tap, tap* continued, the situation became rather eerie.

The spooky noise took a turn to a poltergeist-type haunting. Whenever Bobbie entered her shop to start her day, she found that items and tools had been moved around. Since she was the first one in and last one out of her shop, she knew before leaving everything was in its place. Bobbie believed something unnatural was going on. She thought she got her answer one afternoon after a very hectic morning of framing. She was late on a project and could not get the frame to work correctly. A part was missing. So, in a frustrated moment, she said in a very demanding voice, "Mr. Reich, I know you are here, and from one craftsman to another, can you help me? This frame piece will not work." Immediately, she heard movement in the back area of the shop where she keeps her framing supplies. She continued to head back while calling out, "Is anyone there?" No one responded. What she saw next confirmed her suspicions of the presence of Mr. Reich. The piece of frame that she needed to complete the project was extending from the bind of parts in plain view. She thanked him and finished the job. Bobbie continued after her retirement to correspond with Mr. Reich, the first ghost of our haunted suburb.

Our next haunted tale was experienced next door to the Reich shoemaker shop. The 1880 Grunent/Ruff house and business, last owned by Marilyn Ruff Clemmons, Bobbie's sister, contained a former family spirit. Marilyn was the third-generation family member to live in the home at 612 South Poplar Street. She was also the operator and owner of Ruffs Florist. Marilyn was a second-generation florist who followed her mother and father, Mr. and Mrs. John Ruff Jr., at the same location. Mr. Grunent and his son, Robert, began their own florist shop, West Salem Greenhouse, in the late 1880s in this homestead. Until Marilyn's sudden death in 2014, the florist business had existed in this one house for more than 130 years, one of the longest continuously operating florist businesses in one location in North Carolina.

Mr. and Mrs. Grunent resided and worked most of their lives at 612 South Poplar Street, and it seems Mrs. Grunent may have never left. The Grunent family was part of an early German clan who arrived in the area in the late 1700s. After Marilyn Ruff Clemmons bought the establishment, she often found herself working late alone in the building. Working late one night, she felt someone or something was watching her as she practiced her craft of floral design for the next day's delivery. As she worked, she heard a noise in the hallway, and she watched the entrance door from the hallway with a sideways glance. At first, what she witnessed startled her. A small lady, under five feet tall, was peering at the corner of the door. Marilyn focused on the face, which appeared more solid than a ghostly, see-through shape. Immediately, she knew who the lady was—or *had been*, since she had been deceased several years. The lady she identified as Mrs. Grunent. Marilyn had known the lady since Marilyn was a child growing up next door to the florist shop that was now hers.

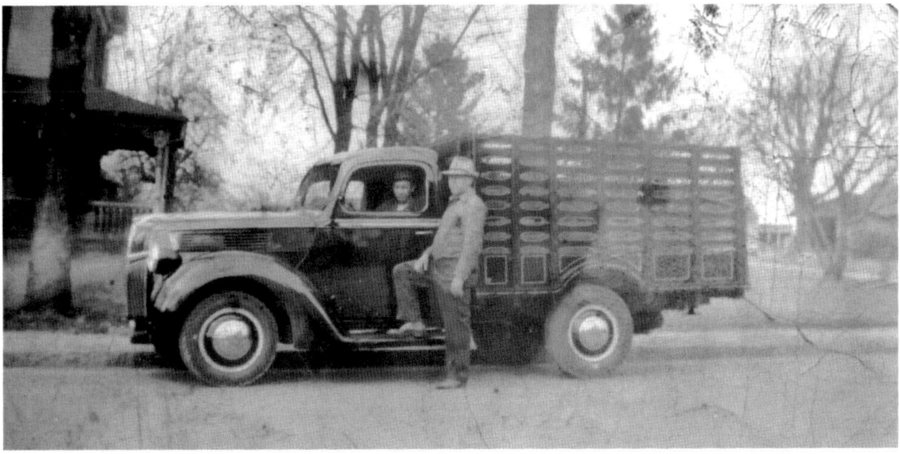

Mr. Joyce, outside of the truck, ran a local grocery store on West Street, and Mr. Grunent, the driver, worked at his dad's flower shop, West Salem Greenhouses. The parsonage of Christ Moravian Church is in background. This circa 1930s photo was taken in front of Mr. Joyce's home at 607 South Green Street.

In the years after her first encounter with the specter, sightings of her became more prevalent not only to Marilyn but also to other members of her family and numerous customers. Customers came in regularly with the hope of spying what the locals called "the spunky little lady who peeps around corners." The apparition could be found peeping around doors and at the top of the flight of stairs that traverses the long hallway from the front door. She has even been spied at the many windows, watching the coming and goings of the family and the customers.

Unfortunately, the old florist shop is closed now. After Marilyn's passing, there was no one to carry on the 130-year florist tradition. Currently, the house is in a state of limbo with regard to its future. The structure has had a lot of wear and tear over the years and is in need of total renovation. If it does not get the help it needs, demolition could be its only option. Hopefully, this historic house, one of the most unique structures on the block, will regain its former glory, maybe even as a florist business once more. I am sure Mrs. Grunent would happily agree.

Our third supernatural experience is at the circa 1854 Tesch/Butner/Bryant/Clemmons home. This was the residence of Marilyn and her husband, Jack Clemmons, owners of Ruffs Florist, before their recent passing. Their daughter, Lane, a fourth-generation Ruff, resides there currently. Located next door to the florist business, the homeplace is a gem within itself. The house is unique in that it sits back from the street farther than any house on the block. The arrangement and configuration of the house is completely different from any other located here. The Old West Salem Historic District Survey explains, "This is a two-story, single bay, front gable, six over six, double hung sash, weather board, and a one-story gabled roof wing, hip roof and a wrap-around porch." Portions of the house were built by Christen David Tesch in 1854; however, the back section of the original house, built farther back from the streetscape, appears to be much older. It is believed, by the historic consultant who documented the survey as well as by the late Marilyn Ruff Clemmons, that the older structure was part of the outbuildings of the early Moravians. Late eighteenth-century structures are still being found throughout the historic district, hidden in later nineteenth- and twentieth-century additions.

The paranormal activity has been experienced by several generations of families, including the Ruffs, the Clemmons and the Bryants. The findings for this supernatural tale point to activity by the spirit of Samuel Butner. Samuel Butner purchased the property in 1865. He was the superintendent of the F&H Fries Cotton Mills. He served as mayor of Salem from 1896 to 1901 and 1903 to 1907. Mr. Butner was very prominent, and during his period as mayor, he used his influence to bring the two parts of the town lot together—literally. Bridges were built between East Salem, Old Salem today, and Old West Salem: the Bank Street Bridge, the West Street Bridge and the Washington Avenue Bridge.

After Mr. Butner's passing, the families who occupied his famous home believed his ghost still walked the halls. The sweet smell of his brand of cigar smoke was experienced late at night after everyone in the house had retired. Boots were heard clomping up and down the stairs of the old structure, and the apparition of the mayor was seen and heard humming throughout the house. Some could almost make out the orator-type voice of Mr. Butner as he strolled the halls. Even today, his voice may still be providing us his wisdom for the twenty-first century.

Chapter 9

THE HAUNTED CITY BLOCK

Our last story depicted a city block complete with history and supernatural activity. The paranormal events presented, I believe, were positive ones. The next tale may have a silver lining to it, but the haunted city block is one dark cloud of evil.

Our previous adventure involved a peaceful, quiet block in Old West Salem. Many tourists to Old Salem from around the country often venture from their tours there to get a glimpse of the other side of Salem, Old West Salem. The first suburb of Salem is usually their destination. The description given of their trip to the 600 block of Poplar Street is typically that it reminded them of a Thomas Kincaid painting—enough said.

Our dark city block is not quaint or picturesque. The northern and western edge of the block lies on the original road to Salem, Old Shallowford Road, constructed circa 1765. Now named West First Street, the southern and eastern edge of this block lies on the original Plank Road, circa the 1840s, which then became New Shallowford Road and is currently known as Brookstown Avenue. If one traverses this block today, one would probably only see blighted, empty lots—a wasteland. This god-forsaken block in the shadow of a brand-new, state-of-the-art apartment complex and the modern BB&T ball field stands like a sore thumb crying for its own revitalization. The plans of the city and developers are well underway to incorporate the block and give it all the positive amenities bestowed on present development downtown and in the BB&T ball field corridor. After our readers experience this next tale of the supernatural involving this city block, you all may join in

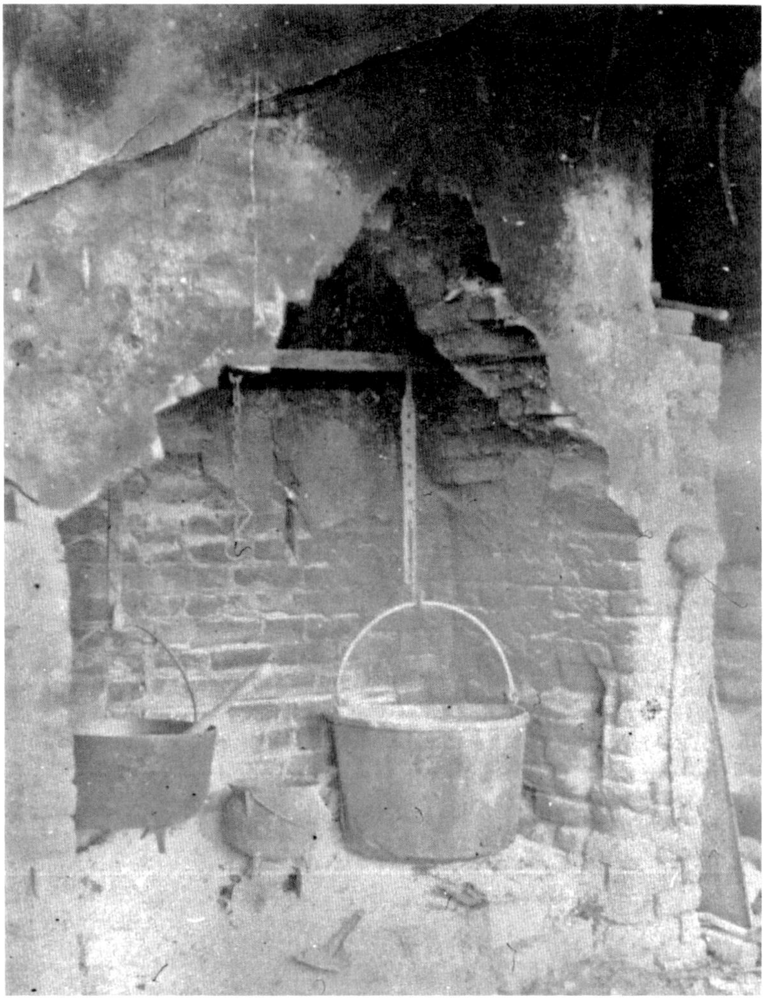

The old fireplace and pot (circa 1818) of the Krueser/Brietz farm is shown. During the 1940s and 1950s, the pot was nicknamed the "cauldron of the Monastery."

with me in my belief that the restorers of the block have their work cut out for them.

The old-timers all agreed when discussing the haunted block. Nearly all the people who lived and worked within this block came to believe the details of the dark past that led to its ultimate demise to a wasteland. The year 2016 marks 250 years of wayfarers who have traveled the Old Shallowford Road, with most coming in contact with the haunted block. The land that made up most of the block existed near the crossroads between Old Salem and Old Winston. Two plantation farms, the Fries farm (circa 1800) and the Krueser/Brietz farm (circa 1816), had their dividing lines to the north and south of the block. In the mid-nineteenth century, the Shutts family located a lumberyard here. They used both slaves and freedmen. The family built homes for these workers within the block, and Shutts Lane was born. After the Civil War, a small pocket neighborhood was developed by African Americans, including a church, a store and a small graveyard. In the late 1880s, it was decided a hospital for the poor was to be built on the Old Plank Road, Brookstown Avenue today.

The Twin City Hospital was constructed circa 1890 on Brookstown Avenue between Shutts Lane, currently the intersection between the avenue and Second Street. The old-timers believed some type of evil force had arrived by way of the Old Plank Road long before the hospital was built, but the hospital and all that went on within the hospital, including the grounds surrounding the institution, seemed to enrich the negative forces within the block. The old-timer Mr. Johns described the evil as similar to the negative energy experienced in the curse of the Fansler Farm in the 1830s by the shaman Running Fox in our earlier tale. Mr. Johns reminds us that conjurers, witches and the like arrived here throughout the heyday of the Great Migration of settlers. The lost graveyard of Shutts Lane could have experienced something similar to that evil curse.

Permit me to clarify something about the lost graveyard before we continue. The Shutts, like the Fanslers, had slaves and freedmen on their farm/plantation. Churches and graveyards were usually a part of the living quarters and surroundings of the African Americans throughout the plantation. When the Twin City Hospital arrived in the late nineteenth century, the old graveyard was already around forty years old. Unfortunately, records, including those of the Shuttses' business ventures, are sketchy in Old Winston history. As an author and historian of local history, I have found the Moravian archives and their history were meticulously recorded and stored, but the Old Winston history, not so much. What is known is that the Twin City Hospital, like most Victorian hospitals of the time, was predominantly for the poor. Wealthy and affluent clients were taken care of at home by doctors who performed house calls. Often, the success rate for patients at early hospitals was not good, and the patients died. The Twin City Hospital budget was tight, and if a patient passed and there was no one to claim the body, the hospital was responsible for the burial. The old-timers had relatives who were associated with the early hospital as nurses and custodians, and the stories told by them were rather macabre. When a patient passed and no

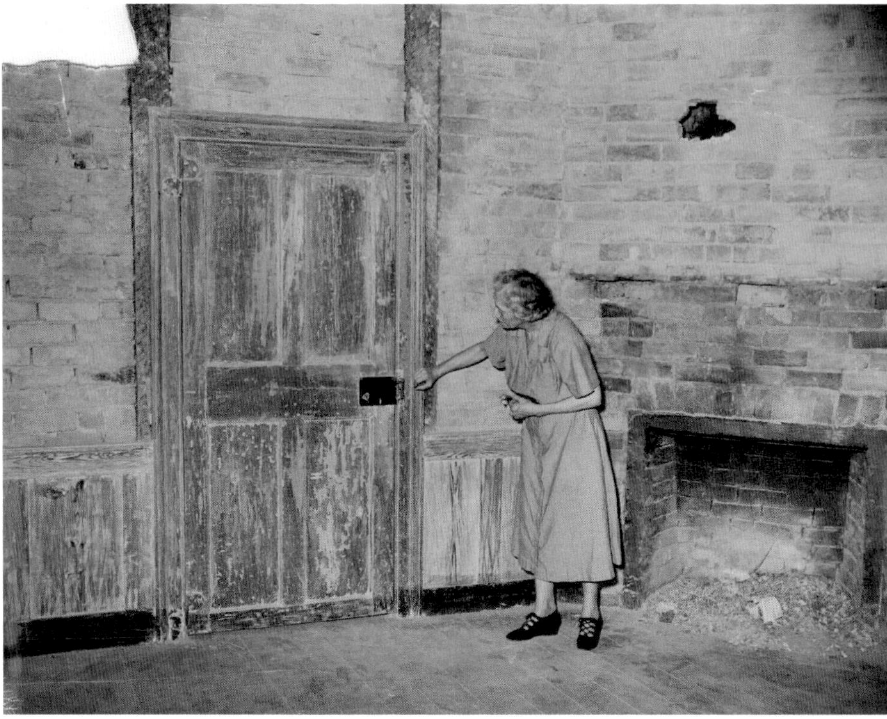

The old brewery of Old West Salem served the town and its occupants well—even the dead ones.

one claimed the body, it was disposed of in or near the African American graveyard. The hospital had taken over the abandoned graveyard that sat behind it, between the church and Shutt Lane. It was reported by locals around the haunted block that the workers at the hospital were frightened and refused to travel near the old graveyard because many bodies of the deceased patients were not always buried in the hallowed ground of the graveyard but elsewhere on hospital property. Plus, the makeshift graves did not have proper coffins or even wooden boxes. Most had no markers or tombstones to identify the dead.

The Twin City Hospital was replaced a mere fifteen years after being constructed by the new City Hospital in East Winston. Supposedly, the Twin City Hospital was to be used as a satellite-type backup, much like the rescue missions and charity hospitals of today.

The evil that had arrived long ago was attracted to the unsanctified graveyard created by the hospital, and literally all hell broke loose. Screams, dark shadows and chaos became the norm for the workers at the hospital and those who lived throughout the block. It had gotten so bad that the leaders of the City Hospital decided to close the branch hospital. A short time later, not only was the hospital abandoned, but parts of the structure were also dismantled. However, what was to happen to the graveyard that seemed to be the center of the block's problems was more sinister. Mysteriously and in the dead of night, the graveyard, along with any trace of it, was dismantled; the headstones and markers disappeared forever.

Mr. Johns related a silver lining to our story:

> *When I think of the small and fragile little girl who touched all who crossed her path, tears well up in my eyes even today, years later. You see, the Twin City Hospital was a pauper hospital, but the last patient that crossed their threshold was a little miracle. I believe she helped to end for a long time the problems generated from the desecrated graveyard. The little angel had showed up to downtown Winston in the teens of 1900. She seemed to live on the street, yet no one knew much about her. Everyone wanted to help her, but she always seemed to help the ones who had tried to assist her much more. Elisabeth was the only name we knew her by. She was Winston's version of the "Little Match Girl." She could brighten your day, even if it was the worst you could possibly have, as she stood in the 400 block of North Liberty Street, the center of town in this time period, selling her wares, matches. She was only eight or nine years of age and was always asked by the adults, "Where are your parents, grandparents, a relative, little one?" Her answer was always the same and always so reassuring: "My father is coming to get me soon." That smile—I can see it as if it was yesterday.*

Mr. Johns began to cry. He continued after a pause:

> *A few weeks later, one bitterly cold December afternoon, I spied Elizabeth on the corner downtown in rags and no shoes. A crowd was around her, and I joined them. "We need to get the little girl a coat and shoes," everyone said. "This could be end of our little angel," they all vocalized. Amazement overcame us all as with what came next. A bright light arose around the little girl as she responded with the softest words: "I am fine. My father will be here shortly." We stayed with little girl until nightfall, but her dad did not come. She became cold as the light around her diminished and went out much like the matches she sold. We rushed her to the City Hospital. They were told she could not pay even though those present wanted to help. We were directed to the Twin City Hospital, and we arrived after dark. Only*

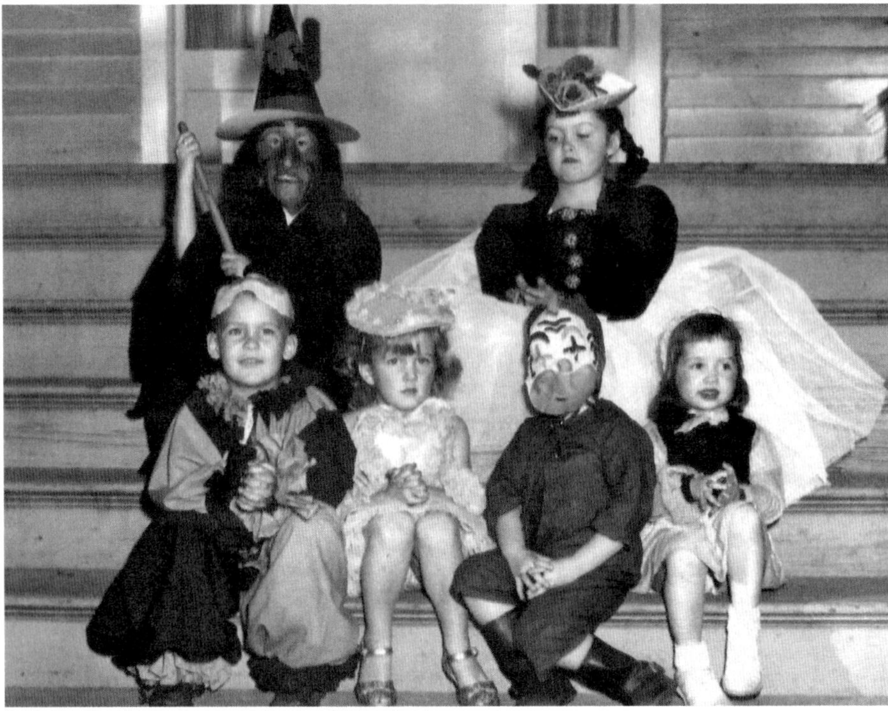

Halloween came into its own in the 1950s and the 1960s, as evidenced by these costumed local children of the city.

one nurse was on duty, and she informed us that all the other patients had been released or, more truthfully, had died. Elizabeth was the last patient of the hospital, forever.

The next day we returned to the hospital to check on Elizabeth. The nurse and the doctor who were on duty told us the horrible news. Elizabeth had passed late in the night. The doctor excused himself, and the nurse explained the strange events of her death. The hour before her demise was described by the nurse: "I had left the patient's room and returned a short time later. The little girl had gotten out of bed and left the premises of the hospital. Something drew me to the window, and there in the field near the old graveyard stood the patient. She was all aglow in the most beautiful light I had ever seen. As a nurse who has witnessed many deaths of patients, this type of occurrence has never happened. I gained my composure, raised the window and hollered to the girl. The cold wind nearly chilled me to the bone. As Elizabeth responded, her words were so calming and reassuring. She smiled and spoke: 'My father has come for me!' A beacon of light as if from Heaven itself surrounded her. The grounds of the old graveyard begin to shake, and I could feel the quakes inside the hospital. The girl's spirit appeared to exit her body along with a multitude of other spirits who exited their graves behind the little one. I knew with all my being she was returning to her father, God, in Heaven."

The crowds of adults were awestruck and proceeded to ask the nurse if she had reported this to the doctor. She responded very directly, "I need my job, so no!" The little angel had returned to her rightful father, and the silver lining to our story was not her death, but the spirits she rescued from the unholy graveyard.

For a time thereafter, the evil was eliminated, and the haunted block was clear. The effects lasted until the 1960s, when the problems returned. Different residences and businesses within the block between Fayette Street and First Street began to experience supernatural events once more. Mysterious lights, screams in the night and ungodly shadows permeated the neighborhood. Most families had to eventually move or abandon their homes. The police were called many times to the block but could not find any physical evidence for these happenings. They told the residents that dealing with metaphysical occurrences was not part of their job description.

I personally had the opportunity to visit the block in the 1980s to attend a Big Brother/Big Sister meeting in one of the few houses that still remained within the block. After the meeting, we stayed and conversed about the goings-on in the old house, since many in attendance—including myself—felt a creepy feeling while there. Those employed were eager to weave their own tales of poltergeist activity there. Things were often moved, shadows were present and invisible touches were felt. No one wanted to stay after dark there, and all were glad the organization would soon move to a new building, far away from the block.

After the move, empty buildings were razed and new construction was attempted. Several projects started in the 1990s, but they only made it to the stage of digging basements. The projects mysteriously stopped before they could complete the basements. Several holes and unfinished grading can be found in this wasteland even today. New construction associated with the ball field projects, including hotels, eateries and businesses, is in the works. I hope that along the way, the evil that once resided here will not be resurrected, but only time will tell.

Chapter 10

The Old Tobacco Wagon Still Rolls

King Tobacco arrived to Winston-Salem in the 1870s. P.H. Hanes, R.J. Reynolds and Brown Brothers were among those who brought tobacco to prominence in Winston-Salem. The old tobacco wagons made by the Nissen and Spach Wagon Works provided the transportation of choice to get the tobacco to market. The old-timers spoke fondly of the two wagons, and their history lesson on these two contraptions went something like this: "The Nissen wagon was quickly plodded and same was true of the Spach wagon. They had a crooked body, kind of shaped like a boat. The 'Neesin' wagon, as we liked to call it, was high-wheeled, forty-two inches in front and fifty-two inches in back. Its running gear was painted a bright, shiny red, the body was green and the char work pure black. It was topped with canvas curved over oak bows. A serviceable machine and my, oh my, pretty too."

Mr. Johns added more history:

> *In the 1830s, the Paper Mill Settlement was alive in the number of settlers who arrived to the Piedmont, drawn here by the gold strike. Many Nissen wagons were purchased then and with the gold strike in California in the 1840s, more wagons were needed to head west for fame and fortune. By 1848, California had rooted out North Carolina as the number one producer of gold. In 1854, Mr. Will Spach had just started his wagon making business and the timing for the business was perfect. The Fayetteville and Winston Plank Road had reached Salem. This opened the way for a big trade that began to flow from the mountains and Piedmont counties to*

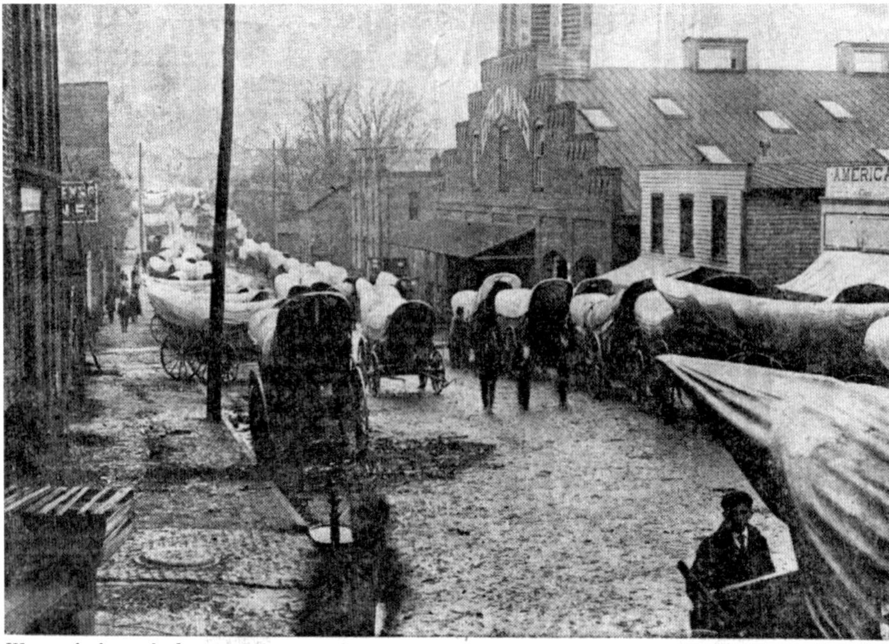

Wagons in front of tobacco warehouses, 1872.

The old Nissen wagons were a mainstay at the tobacco market circa 1872.

> *the coast. That trade moved in wagons, whole freight trains of Nissen and Spach wagons. It also had a trade in whiskey and brandy, I believe, if recollections serve me. A Nissen wagon was built just wide enough to accommodate three keys, side by side, in roots like ginsey, herbs like penny royal oil, sassafras, Seneca snake root, dried fruits, honey and beeswax, chestnuts, ham and bacon, hides and talons, buckwheat and flaxseed. With the onslaught of the Civil War, Nissen and Spach wagon sales to the Confederates skyrocketed.*

The old-timers had to add a quote from their school days, "The Confederation of Johnny Rebs were dressed in Fries cotton uniforms and traveled in Nissen and Spach wagons, all home grown in Winston-Salem!"

In her book *Bright Leaf*, Nannie M. Tilley, an expert in R.J. Reynolds Tobacco history, explained the importance of the wagon:

> *So essential were Nissen wagons in marketing tobacco that they have been deemed a decisive factor in the development of the bright leaf tobacco industry throughout the entire Piedmont region. By the 1870s,*

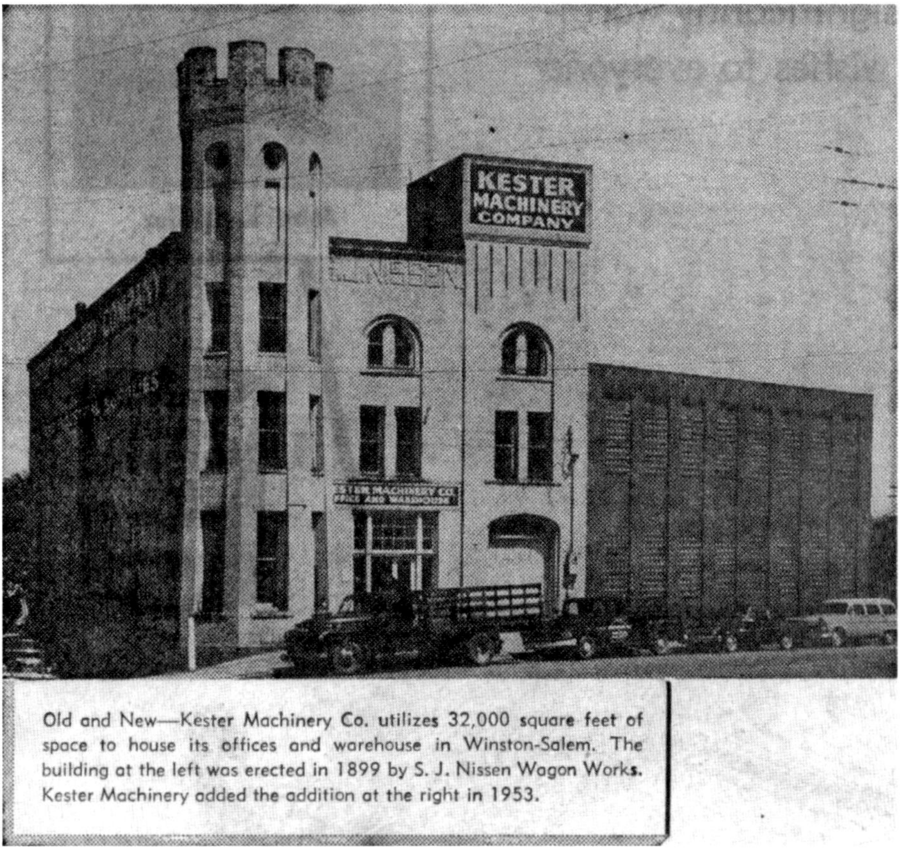

Kester Machinery (circa the 1890s) was a major company in Old Winston.

> *the new bright leaf was being planted in ever-growing quantities in the Old Belt. Men like Washington Duke and his son, Buck, Dick Reynolds and Pleus Hanes spread the fame of the new bright leaf when they peddled their plug tobacco in Nissen and Spach wagons up and down the entire South. The farmers who planted the new leaf used those wagons at market-time.*

Old tobacco wagons could be found everywhere across Winston-Salem, the state of North Carolina and the United States. These were the physical varieties; however, our two tales do not concern the physical but rather the supernatural. Our first tale played out in the 1880s. When the paper mill burned in the late 1870s, the rock quarry closed not long after. The sawmill was moved farther south of the site. It is amazing that the Paper

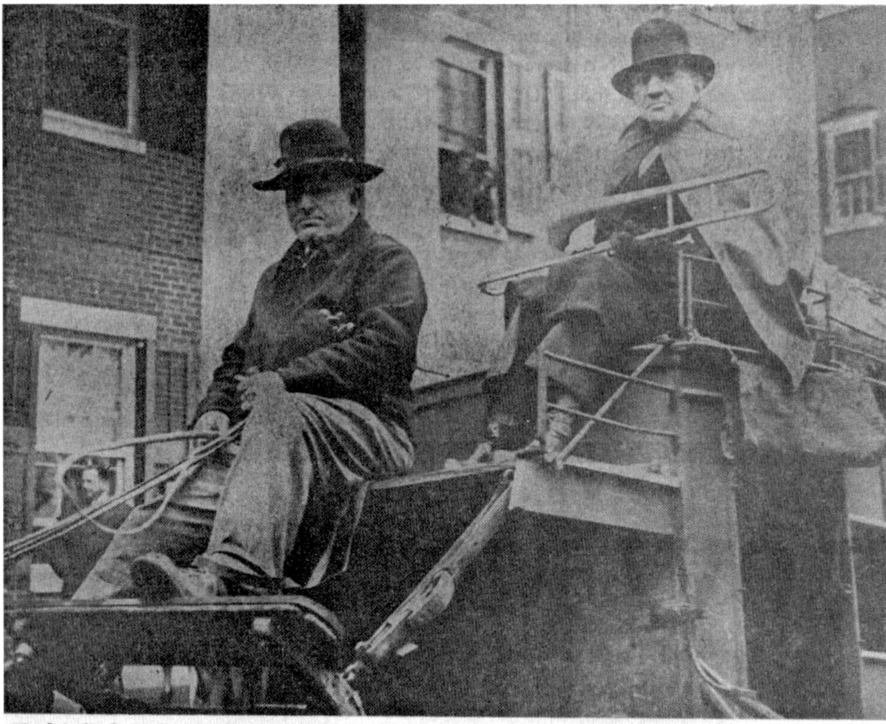

The late B. J. Pfohl, who lead the Moravian Band for years, rides atop an old coach driven by Ed Anderson during Forsyth County's 1949 Centennial celebration.

The old stagecoach with Brother Pfohl at the reins in this 1949 celebration parade of the 100th anniversary of the founding of Winston.

Mill Settlement, which had been a central player, had all been forgotten and had returned to nature. It became a place for locals to hike, camp, hunt and have Sunday picnics.

One dark and chilly night in late autumn, a lone hunter with his two old dogs was on the trail of a rascal of a raccoon. They lost the racoon that night, but they received the experience of a lifetime. The night was pitch black. There was no moon. The hunter recounted later that the autumn air was strange. Instead of feeling refreshing and invigorating, the air was stale and stifling. He thought that since he was in the bottom of Peters Creek, the air should have been cool and moving. The two bloodhounds had lost the scent in the dead air and began to act strange and somewhat scared. He had never seen the dogs act this way before. He was about to call it a night when something occurred, something that he would not have believed in his wildest dreams.

Directly above him, near the remnants of the burned-out mill (in today's landscape, Academy Street above Peters Creek), the ridge was ablaze, not with fire but with light, music and people. His two dogs had had enough and were high-tailing it home to Old West Salem. Unfortunately, the hunter could not follow his hounds because he literally was unable to move. He was paralyzed, not with fear, but he simply could not move physically. He was always a rather levelheaded man, and he wanted to climb the ridge to see what all the commotion was about. Shortly, he realized all this celebration was not his to enjoy or to take part in. The hunter tried again to move and was only able to turn his head to look behind. In the background, he found music not on the creek but on a fancy bridge over it. Suddenly, fear overcame him. Wagons, people, horses and oxen were headed straight at him from the bridge. He was sure he was going to be trampled, but the entities passed through him as if he was not there at all. The entire group proceeded into the darkness beyond the light that had encircled the beautiful bridge. In an instant, as if nothing had happened, the hunter found himself standing at the creek in total darkness. It was pitch black, and his two dogs were by his side. As he and his dogs left the creek bank and headed home, he turned for one last look at the magical bridge. He then realized what he had experienced and what would be experienced years later by others. A large wagon train that emitted its own light source was traveling in a line up the old Paper Mill Road. Its destination was west with new settlers to find their new homes in the United States territories of old. Nearly one hundred years after the physical entities had taken the same journey, the supernatural ones were experiencing theirs.

Tobacco wagons were probably not included with the hunters' vision of the past. However, I had a personal experience with a tobacco wagon of another time. During the time period I spent with the old-timers at the Green Front Cash Store, my first supernatural experience occurred. My residence was 119 South Broad Street, the former home of the doctor who ran the sanatorium of Forsyth County. By 1960, Broad Street at the intersection of Old Shallowford Road had been the site of comings and goings for nearly two hundred years. All forms of transportation had traversed this road—be it dirt, sand, plank, macadam or asphalt.

My encounter with the unknown in 1961 came by way of this road. Beginning in late September, usually early in the morning on Saturdays, I was awoken by a strange noise, one I had never heard before. I asked my grandmother, who was the early riser at the homeplace, to identify the sounds I had heard. Her eyes brightened, and a small grin appeared on her face. She stated, "You must have heard the tobacco man and his wagon." She told me the story of years ago, when the tobacco farmers from all over Forsyth County brought their tobacco to market during the fall. They came by way of the older roads of Winston-Salem, and of course, Broad Street was one of the main ones.

"Do the old tobacco wagons still roll even now?" I asked.

She answered, "The market is still strong on Trade Street downtown at the Old Farmers Tobacco Warehouse. However, now trucks are the choice transportation."

This did not explain the reason I heard the old wagon sound that day. My grandmother Mary explained with a grin, "You have just heard a haint!"

I had heard the expression from the old-timers at the grocery store. "A haint? You mean a ghost?" I asked.

"Yes, and if you get up next Saturday, very early with me, you may see the haint as well!" she answered. That next Saturday, I saw the first ghost of my life. From the second story on the side porch of 119 South Broad Street, I had my first experience with an apparition. A small farmer, dressed in bib overalls, had a Nissen wagon loaded with tobacco headed up Broad Street directly in front of my house. My grandmother was standing beside me during this whole ordeal. I told her I was going down to confront this so-called haint. She responded by saying, "Good luck to that; I have tried several times but to no avail."

But before she could get those words out of her mouth, I had already made it downstairs and was exiting the front door. I even ran a couple blocks toward town, the direction the old haint had headed, but the man and the wagon had disappeared. I tried several more times to catch up to this haint over the fall season, but without success.

The landscape has changed at the old crossroads of Broad and First Streets over the fifty years since I first saw the haint. However, the locals still swear that if you can get up early enough on a cool autumn day—preferably on Saturday—you, too, may get a look at the old tobacco wagon as it still rolls.

Chapter 11

Salem Cemetery Horror

Salem Cemetery began as an extension of Gods Acre, the Moravian graveyard established circa 1771. After the arrival of the town of Winston in 1849, the county seat of the newly created Forsyth County, Salem Cemetery was born in 1850. Unlike the Moravian graveyard that was solely for the Moravian church and its members, Salem Cemetery was more diverse and evolved as the town of Winston grew. The movers and shakers of Winston bought up many of the plots there. The tobacco, cotton and mercantile business owners and the like constructed large, impressive buildings to showcase their business prowess, and in death, their tombstones, crypts and mausoleums were just as impressive dotting the cemetery's landscape. Even several of the Moravians entrepreneurs—Fries, Belos, Shaffner—had purchased resting places within its borders.

Salem Cemetery was an example of the resting places that appeared in growing towns and cities of the mid-nineteenth century. The Industrial Revolution was well underway, and the grandeur that was fitting for the business elites and all their accomplishments in life had to be presented in death as well. If one travels through the gates of God's Acre and studies the rows and rows of organized gravestones of the Moravians, the Salem Cemetery monoliths create a definite contrast. Where God's Acre is a smooth, rolling hillside home of the dearly departed, Salem Cemetery contains steep hills and ravines—a landscape our readers are accustomed to from earlier tales. This may have had an influence on the horror that found its way to Salem Cemetery instead of God's Acre.

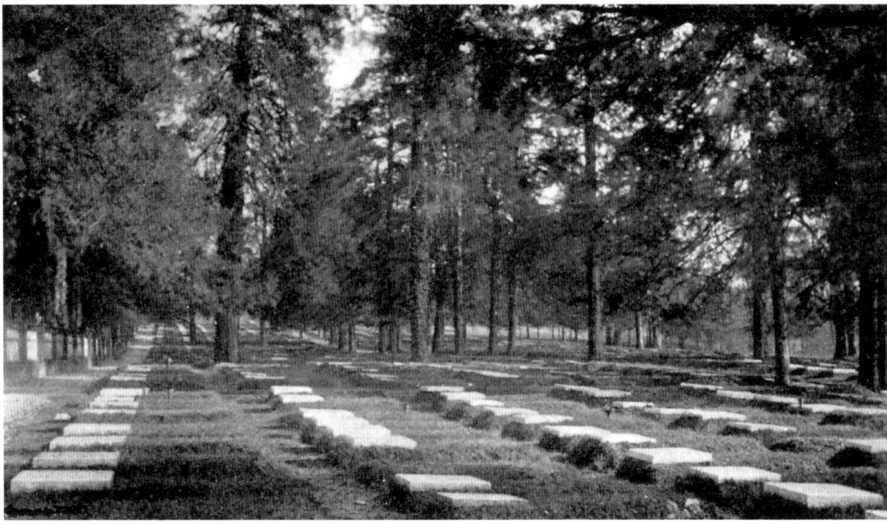

Salem Cemetery, seen in this photograph circa 1920.

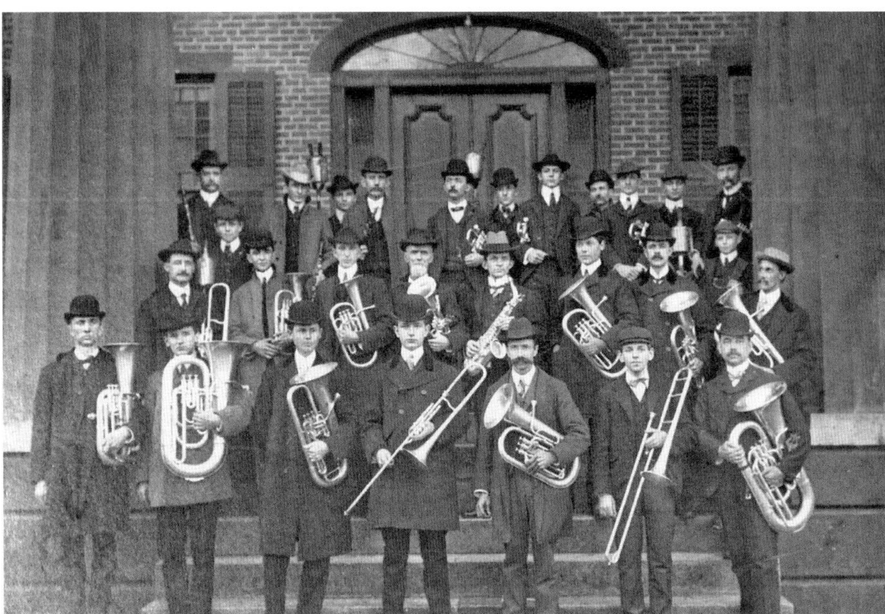

The Salem Band in a 1914 photo.

Our gruesome tale begins a few years after Salem Cemetery was created and Winston was just becoming the bustling county seat of Forsyth County, with all of its positive and negative attributes. The conservative Moravians wanted no part of a county seat town, with drunks and loafers congregating on court days. The whipping post, a legal punishment for many offenses, graced the courthouse square, macabre yet functional. In addition, the Prison House was another fixture of gloom and doom, as stated by the *Peoples Press* newspaper in 1851: "Then comes the Prison House—not yet completed, rather a gloomy looking place. May the mere sight of its grated windows prove a terror to evildoers and its cells ever remain tenantless?"

Tenantless it was not. Several indoor hangings were performed over the lifetime of the prison. The Moravians were right about the drunks at court time. The Winston town board finally passed a law that anyone found drunk on the street was to be punished by no fewer than thirteen but no more than thirty-nine lashes. The old-timers reported that the whipping post stayed rather busy; the punisher who administered the whippings was not good with arithmetic, to the detriment of the criminals. The whipping post was a key factor to our tale.

Between the courthouse square and the location of Salem Cemetery, an event occurred that connected the dots of our story with the infamous whipping post. In 1854, the Fayetteville and Western Plank Road was finished, and Winston was off to its first boom. The Plank Road came right through Salem and Winston up Main Street, the location of the courthouse. The Fries family, owners of the textile mill, persuaded the builders of the Plank Road to create a spur to his cotton factory, at Fries's expense, on New Shallowford Road (Brookstown Avenue today). The spur continued past the mill and dead-ended into South Main Street. Mysteriously, at the dead end of Main Street existed a small walkway that led directly into God's Acre and, from there, connected to a path to Salem Cemetery.

The Plank Road was an interesting experiment in pre-railway transportation, and it played an important part in Winston's early development. The plank road was built of timbers, laid lengthwise, with a roadbed of cross planks. The planks were not nailed down, and wagons must have made a terrible noise as they rolled through the small town.

The courthouse square looked like a circus had arrived to the town in the late 1850s when county court was in session, and the whipping post was cleared and ready for action. A motley crew of drunks, swindlers, gamblers and ladies of the night, so-called by the old-timers, was in attendance. Once

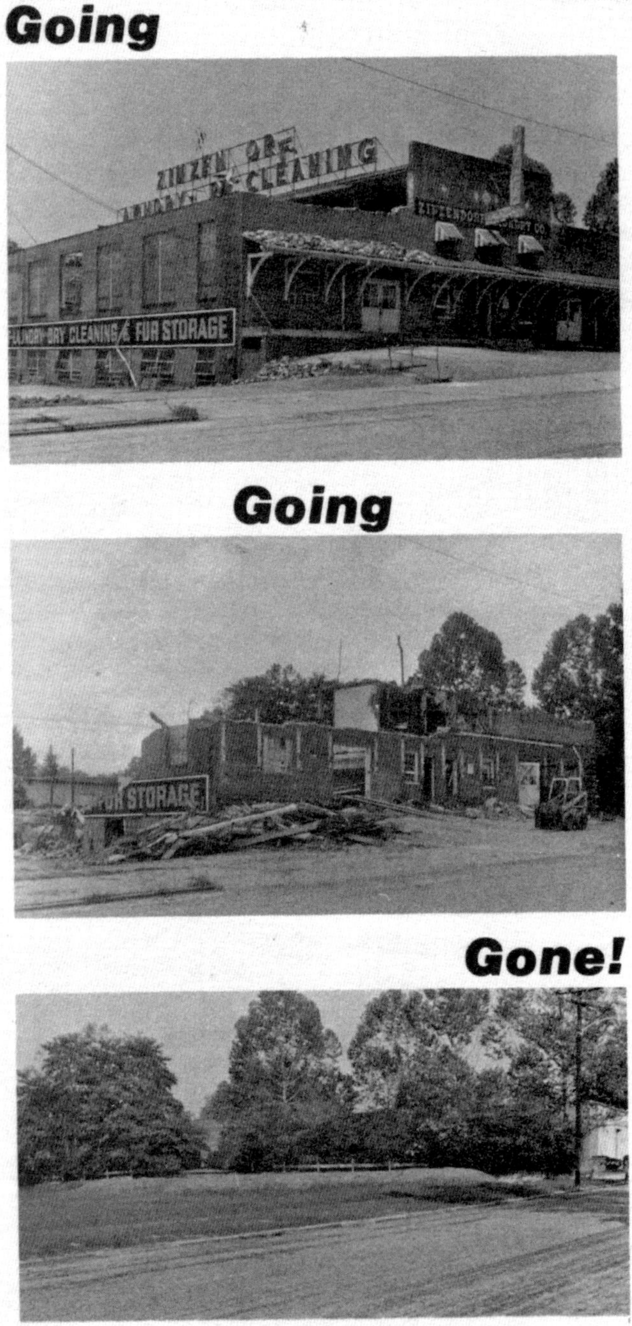

ZINZENDORF LAUNDRY

The Zinzendorf Laundry received its name from Count Von Zinzendorf, the protector of the early Moravians in Europe, and this image depicts its razing by Old Salem. The location was near the current bridge and walkway of Old Salem Center.

the court cases were tried and the judge gave the final verdicts and penalties, the dark entertainment would begin.

One particular court day, the snap of the whip was heard hundreds of times. However, one of the participants did not go gently into the good night afterward. The old-timers simply called the woman the unwanted guest of Winston, not because of her conviction but of what happened after her death. The woman was not a drunk or a lady of the night. She was simply insane, according to the onlookers who experienced her tirade. Before her punishment was delivered, the guest began to ramble loudly in what appeared to be in an unknown tongue, according to the clergy in attendance. Suddenly, she spoke in a more fluent English and stated that a curse on the town would follow if her punishment was executed. The woman screamed, moaned and continued ranting in the unknown tongue as the punishment was rendered. The circus atmosphere of the court square was silenced when the final strap was laid on the back of woman. Those of the court and onlookers realized the now silent guest of the court was dead.

The old-timers said what happened next was not carried in the newspapers but was only spoken of in a tight circle of officials in the town. The deceased woman was whisked away in a city wagon down the old plank road, *clippety-clop, clippety-clop* across the planks, headed south toward her final resting place. The stranger's graveyard of the Salem Cemetery was the location of her quiet service, with no one in attendance from the town and no marker from the city. The old-timers believed no pine box was present either.

A month passed, and so did the memories of the event by the people of the town. Those involved spoke of the event only as a bad dream.

The cemetery began to experience strange sounds, glowing lights and shadows passing throughout the strangers' graveyard and beyond to the rest of the cemetery. For more than a year afterward, families who had funerals and burials often encountered spooky and weird occurrences during the services of their loved ones. Many mourners swore the ghost of the old insane woman who had died at the whipping post attended several burials of loved ones. The woman wore a smirk on her face and always repeated these words: "They are with me now, and all of you will never see them again." She would then cackle insanely and disappear, leaving the mourners frantic. Along with these occurrences, screams and moans late at night became deafening to the residents around the cemetery. The actions became so disruptive that those who owned plots in the cemetery were threatening the city that they were going to sell their plots and find another cemetery in which to bury their loved ones. The old-timers relayed: "The elders and the city leaders moved swiftly and exhumed the body of the unwanted guest, and moved her to another graveyard near the town of Liberty." The town of Liberty was located between Winston and Walkertown. In today's landscape, if one follows Liberty Street north of downtown to the second old railroad bridge, where White Street used to reside, one would be at the location of the graveyard.

Salem Cemetery was "peaceful" from that day forward. However, the graveyard at White Street where the woman was entombed was relocated in the early 1900s. Some say it was to make way for the new railway spur to Winston. The old-timers believed there may have been more supernatural reasons for the cemetery removal at the last stop for the old woman and the Salem Cemetery horror.

Chapter 12

An Occurrence at the Masonic Temple

The beginning of the twentieth century looked promising for both Winston and Salem. After the great fire had destroyed the Zinzendorf Resort Hotel in 1891, two important decisions were made by the leaders of both cities. The first was that no building of any size would ever again be constructed completely of lumber. The rambling, wooden Victorian structures of the late nineteenth century were labeled fire hazards in growing cities and towns across America. Brick, stone and iron would become the builders' choice for the new monoliths that would dot the landscape in the first twenty years of the twentieth century. Secondly, and locally, any large buildings would be confined to the central downtown section of Winston.

The central character in our haunting tale is one of these first structures, built in 1906. Many years ago, the *Winston-Salem Journal* newspaper did a piece to commemorate the founding of Winston in 1849. An article listed accomplishments of the city for each year. For the year 1906:

> *The Carnegie Public Library opens at the corner of Third and Cherry Street. The large B.F. Huntley Furniture Company is organized on Patterson Avenue, and so is the YWCA on Second Street. The R.J. Reynolds Tobacco Company began to produce a new blend of smoking tobacco that became their best seller, Prince Albert. The Winston-Salem Mutual Life Insurance Company, the first major business venture attempted by Negroes in Winston, is organized. The Chatham*

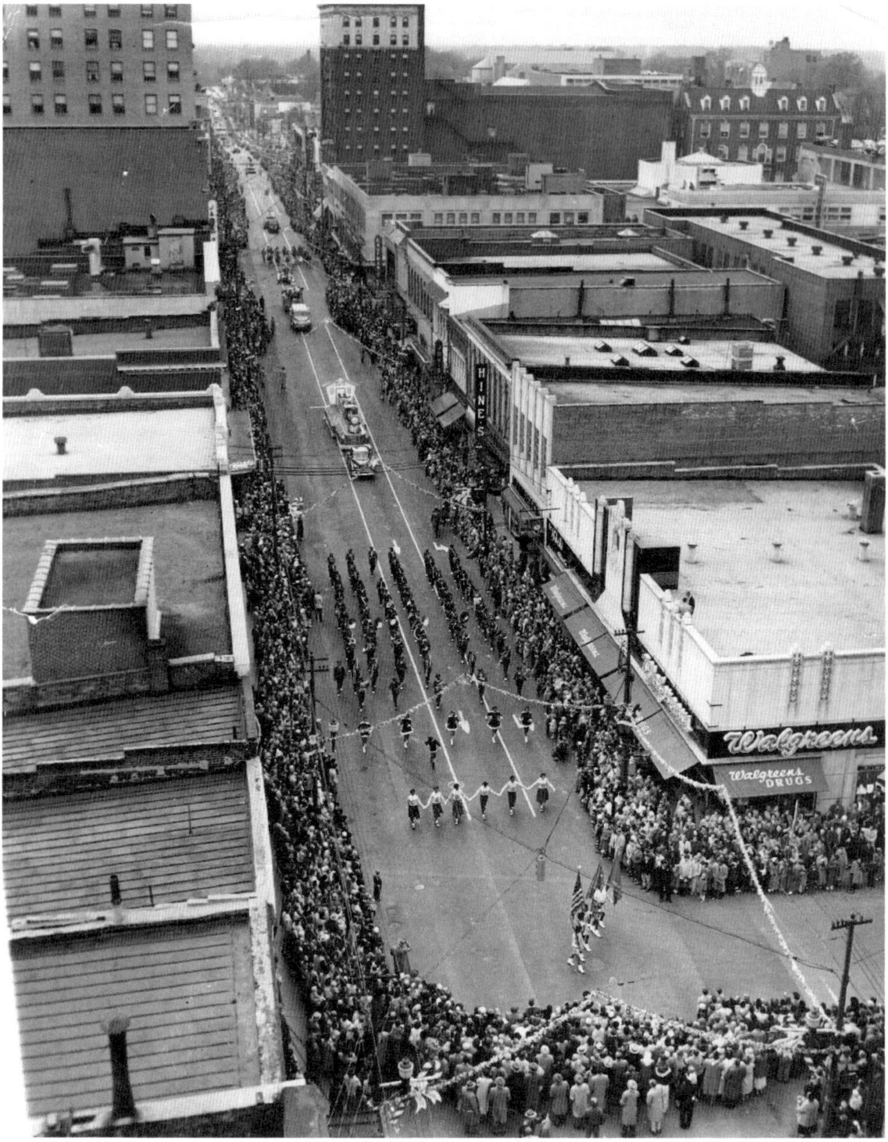

The Twin City Club, located downtown at West Fourth Street and Marshall Street circa 1900, was the meeting place of the business leaders.

Manufacturing Company opens a large plant on Chatham Road in Winston. The stone masons impressive Masonic Temple is built at the corner of Trade Street and West Fourth Street.

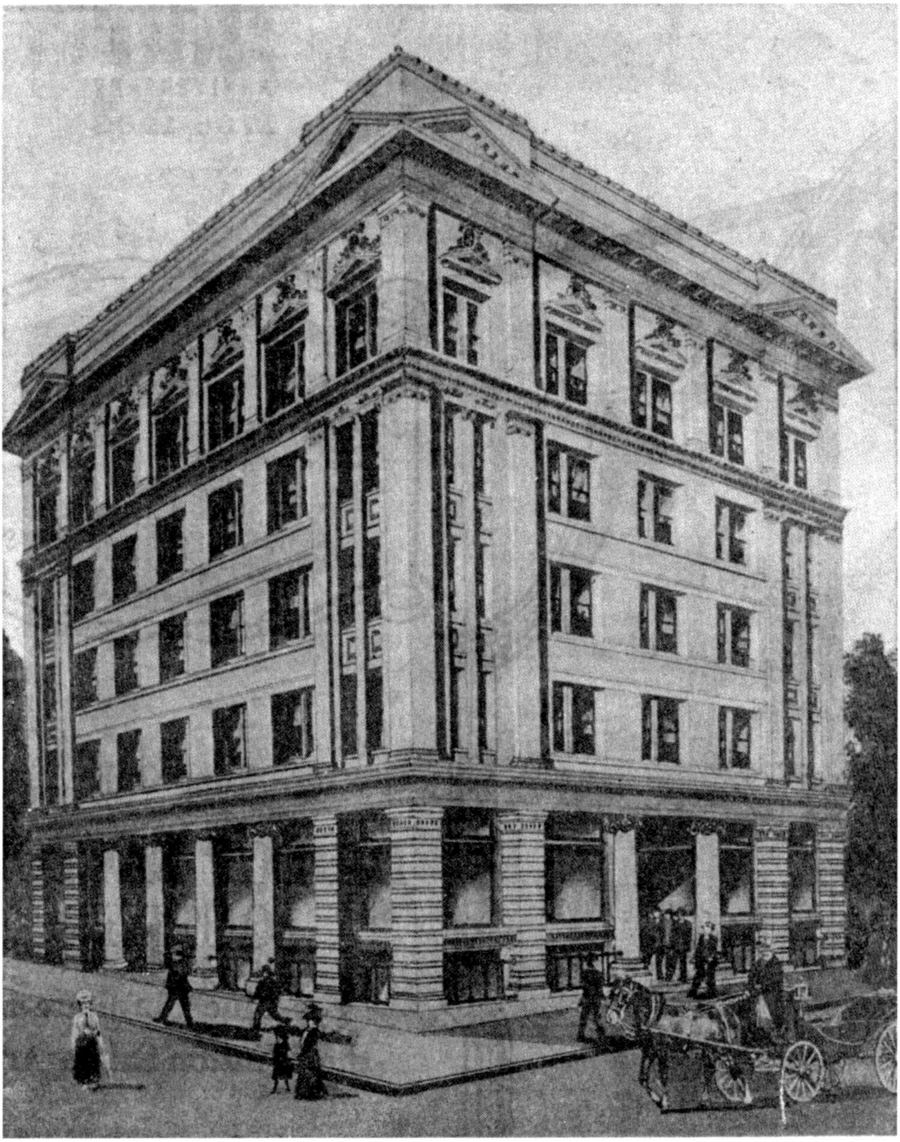

The infamous Masonic Temple, seen here circa 1908.

The Masonic Temple was erected by the masons as a combination office building and lodge hall. Built of granite blocks, it was described at the time as one of the most modern office buildings ever constructed in the state. The building was planned to "last the test of time." The stonework was praised by all the masons locally and all other masons who visited Winston just to

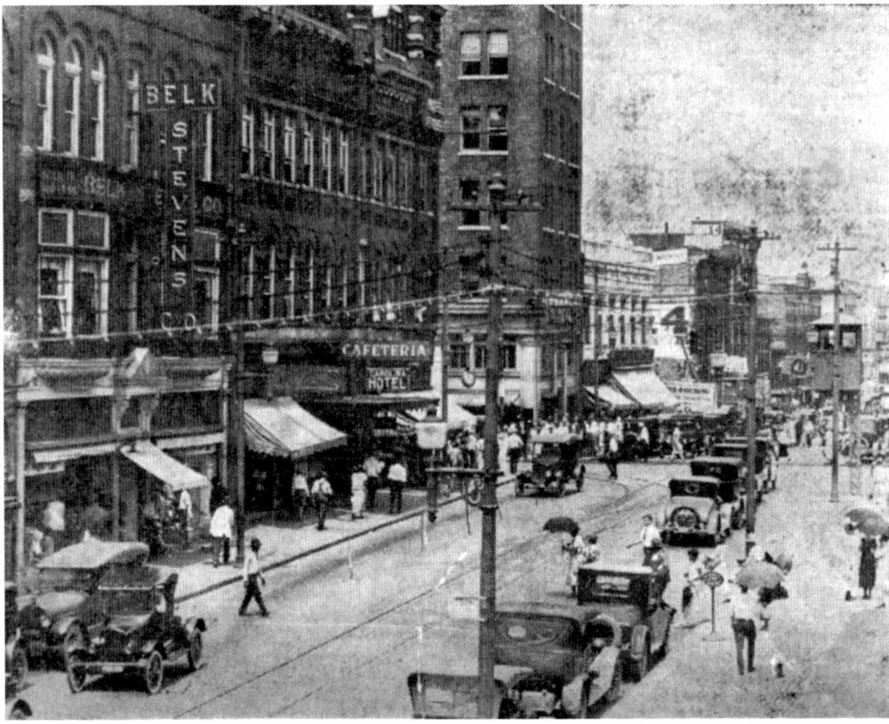

The commerce center at Liberty Street and West Fourth Street, depicted here in the 1920s, contained the Phoenix Hotel (circa 1890), the O'Hanlon Building (circa 1910), the Pre-K&W Cafeteria (circa 1900) and Belk-Stevens (circa 1900).

study this structure with the hope of constructing a similar quality product in their respective towns and cities.

Mysteriously, in 1926, only twenty short years after the temple opened, the Masonic Temple, built to last the test of time, was razed and destroyed. The granite blocks that had been honed by the stonemasons were dispersed over Forsyth County. To this day, these blocks can still be found across the backyards of residents of the county. The reason given to the citizens, who believed this destruction to be an atrocity and a waste, appeared in a byline in the *Winston-Salem Journal*: "The owners of the temple and the city officials of 1926 have determined its usefulness is over and the structure should be terminated."

This made absolutely no sense; the leaders of the city had determined new growth was coming to Fourth Street by way of the Roaring Twenties. A building boom was underway in 1925 to create what the city called the "Great White Way." It ran from Fourth Street at Main Street west along

Fourth Street to the West End School at Fourth and Broad Streets. Tall buildings, our city's version of skyscrapers, were to line up in a "Great White Way" of light and progress down Fourth Street. This would create the most modern mix of office buildings in the state. The Masonic Temple was the tallest office building on Fourth Street until the Nissen Building was built in 1926. The temple was razed that same year and replaced by the Art Deco Walgreens Drug Company building the same year. The drugstore was a plain, one-story structure at a key location of the Great White Way of light, at the corner of Fourth and Trade Streets. The masons moved to several locations throughout the city, never having a building of their own until the 1950s, when they relocated to Miller Street in the Ardmore neighborhood. This was a one-story facility and, as of this writing, has been razed for a new grocery store under construction.

The mystery of the Masonic Temple may seem strange, but you may not consider it a sinister paranormal event. This is where you would be wrong. The paranormal occurrence at the temple begins in 1925 with the vision of one mason who was known by the old-timer Mr. Johns. The mason was closing up shop at the Temple one cold and eerie night. As the man checked the locks on the door, a strange foreboding feeling came over him. As he was walking away from the Temple, headed west up Fourth Street, a strange feeling caused him to turn and glance back at the building. The vision he saw made the Mason question his own sanity. The Masonic Temple had changed, and strange banners hung from the windows of the Temple and over the entry door. Several strange flags hung from the eves of the building, encircling it. As if by magic, the scene changed, and the light of day shone on the building and surrounding landscape. Visible now were men and women in strange attire, somewhat military in appearance, with the same symbols on their uniforms as were displayed on the banners and flags on the building. The Mason heard muffled sound as the entities spoke to one another in a language he did not recognize. The Mason gained his composure and walked back to the temple. As quickly as the vision appeared, it vanished. The cold wind gave him a chill, and the darkness brought him back to the reality of the night. Mr. Johns related, "The Mason was a sane human being—and a teetotaler at that." The Mason shared his vision with his fellow Masons at the next meeting. To his surprise, other Masons had seen similar visions but were somewhat afraid to share with anyone because they thought no one would believe them. The Masonic Elders, however, differed since the ritual of their forebearers traced back centuries, with clairvoyance and occult knowledge being at the forefront of their training in different degrees of Masonship.

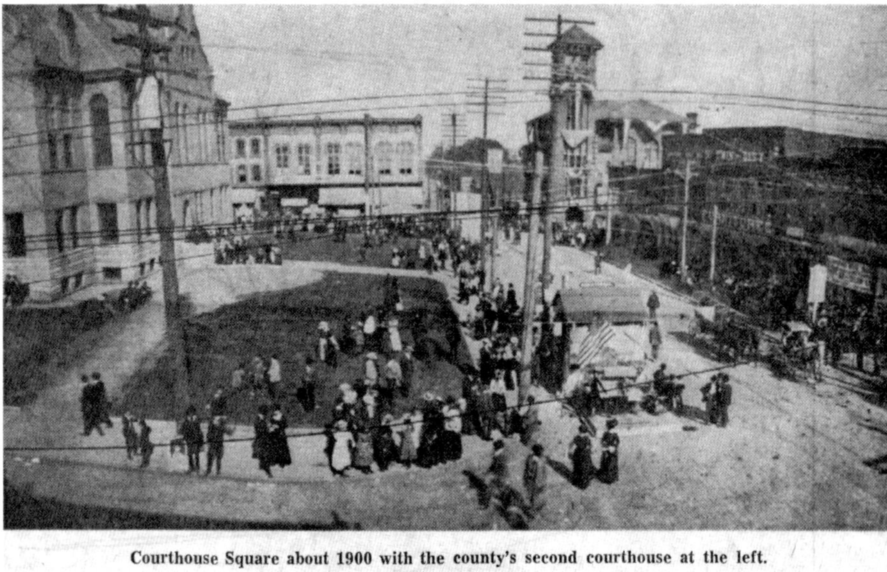

The courthouse block circa 1900, looking north at the new 1896 courthouse (the Castle).

The Mason Elders met for more than a week in secret to discuss and meditate over their Masonic knowledge for answers. Their findings revealed a horror too terrible to express to anyone outside their immediate circle. The Mason Elders brought their horrible answers of their visions to the National Fraternal Order of the Masons and found they were not the only branch of Masons to express the vision. With a downtrodden appearance and a lump in his throat, Mr. Johns spoke to all those who were at the Green Front Cash Store that night and explained the findings of the Masonic Elders. Their findings provided an answer that would change the landscape of the Masonic Temple block forever. These are Mr. Johns's words:

> *When my friend, the Mason, explained his vision and how the Masonic Elders had deciphered the mystery of the vision, I shivered with fear in this vision. The men and women along with the banners of flags were part of an omen of the evil that was coming to America if that evil was not stopped. The symbols and all concerned would be America's future if not stopped. The Masonic Elders decided the power generated and the occult knowledge found in the stone built Masonic Temples across America led to the dismantlement of the structures in order to stop the*

> *evil from gaining the power. If the vision of evil was allowed to tap the Masonic Temple's power, it could allow the future entities to rule the world.*

Many historians believe the Masonic Temple was taken down, as were many others across America at this time period. I believe our readers would agree with me when I say that the occurrence at the Masonic Temple created a vision of horror that, if allowed to continue, would have became America's future—a future of Nazism, the Third Reich of Germany.

Chapter 13

The Last Picture Show

Entertainment has existed in Winston-Salem since the first Moravian brethren arrived in Salem in 1766. Moravian music and their bands are known throughout the world. Vaudevillian performers arrived to the town in the early twentieth century to play at the Elks auditorium circa 1903. Minstrel and comedy shows with local talent like the Forsyth Riflemen also performed. The auditorium burned in the 1910s, but it was replaced by the State Theater, which featured silent and talkie movies and stage shows featuring cowboys, Indians and serial shorts. The Amuza Theater, the premium silent movie house in the area, opened in 1910. The likes of John Barrymore, Lon Chaney, Hoot Gibson and Rudolph Valentino were seen on screen while an organ player provided the sound.

More theaters arrived to the downtown in the 1920s and later, including the Carolina, Forsyth, Winston, Colonial and Paramount. These were the movie theaters that entertained Winston-Salem throughout most of the twentieth century, and all of these listed were attended by white residents only before desegregation arrived to the city in the 1960s. Downtown in the 1920s, African Americans were restricted to east of Main Street. Much of the downtown was bordered by East Fourth Street, East Third Street, Chestnut Street and Depot Street (Patterson Avenue today). Three of the African American movie theaters were found in the downtown block: the Rex, the Lafayette and the Lincoln.

Growing up in Winston-Salem of the 1950s and 1960s, I had many experiences with the movie houses mentioned above. Other than the silent

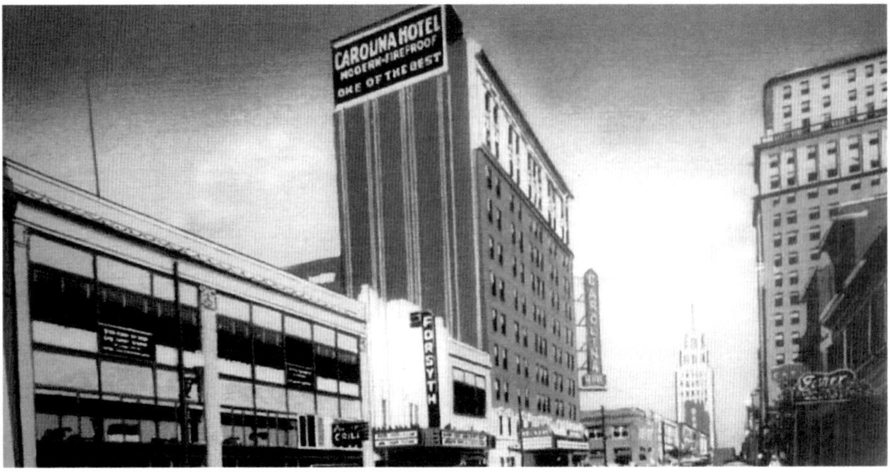

A 1920s postcard of the Forsythe Theater with the Carolina Hotel next door.

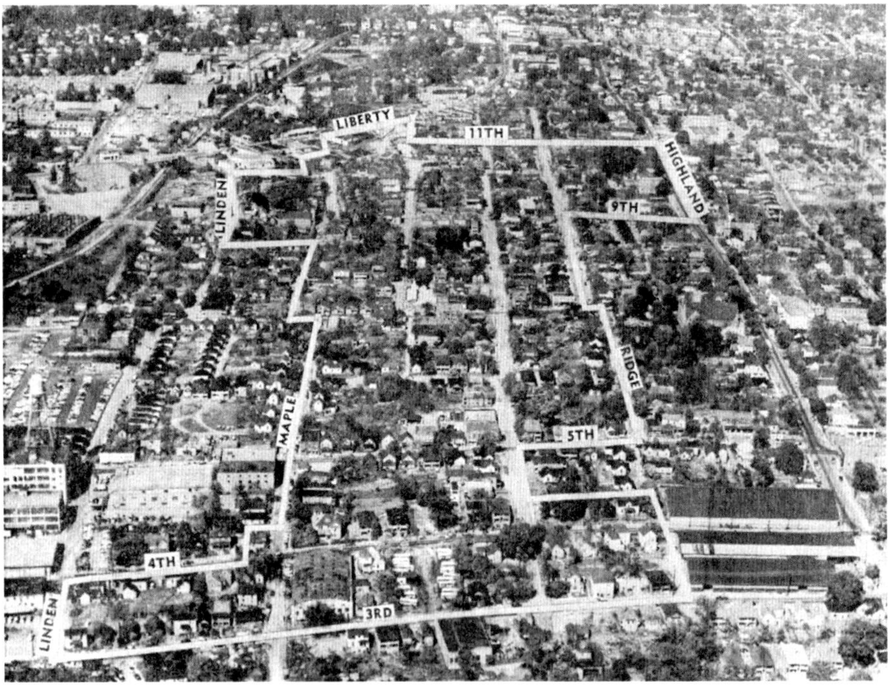

Aerial photo circa 1960s of East Winston, an early neighborhood of Old Winston and home to the Lincoln and Laffite Theaters. The photo was taken just before urban renewal would change the neighborhood forever.

movie houses, the Colonial Theater had become the Center Theater and the Forsyth Theater had been torn down and replaced by the Woolworth's Five and Dime. I patronized them all. The Center Theater was a unique experience since it was the first I attended in the late 1960s with African Americans in attendance. If I may say, some of my favorite memories include going to this theater as a teenager. The African American manager of the theater made some of the best hotdogs and chili in town.

Our tale concerns a haunting experience that occurred one bone-chilling, icy February Sunday night in 1969 at the African American theater the Lincoln. Two friends and I had planned on attending our favorite, the Center Theater, but the icy conditions on the road caused a cancellation of its 9:00 p.m. feature. We were teenagers and were determined to attend a movie that evening. We had always wanted to go to the Lafayette or Lincoln Theater since we had heard so much of its long history. Some adults told us that vaudevillian acts and silent movies had played there since most of the very old silent and vaudevillian theaters of the white residents were all gone. The Lafayette and Lincoln Theaters were unique in that they had not been updated like the other theaters in the city and had more original seating and equipment, the same as in vaudevillian and silent days.

So, we literally ice skated in our tennis shoes down East Fourth Street to the location. Upon arriving, we saw the block was being razed. My friend said this was because of urban renewal in the city. The Lafayette had already been torn down, but the Lincoln was still intact. We walked up to the ticket window, which appeared to be a booth probably dating to the silent era of films. The movie profiled on the marquee was one we wanted to see. The film was titled *Robinson Crusoe on Mars*, a 1968 science fiction flick loosely adapted from the classic *Robinson Crusoe*.

We had to see it, so we asked the African American gentlemen in the booth if there was to be a 9:00 p.m. showing. He was somewhat reluctant to sell us tickets, but he said, "Yes, there is a 9:00 p.m. showing." We asked about the demolition going on, and he replied that this show would be the last show for this theater—forever. The next day, the wrecking ball would claim another victim on the block, and these historic structures would become history. As we rounded the corner of the booth, the man said to us, "Be careful." We looked at each other strangely, and I said, "We've come this far, there is no turning back."

We ventured into the lobby. The snack area was closed and, from the looks of it, had been for a while now. There were two entrances into the theater, to the left and to the right of the snack counter. As we proceeded through

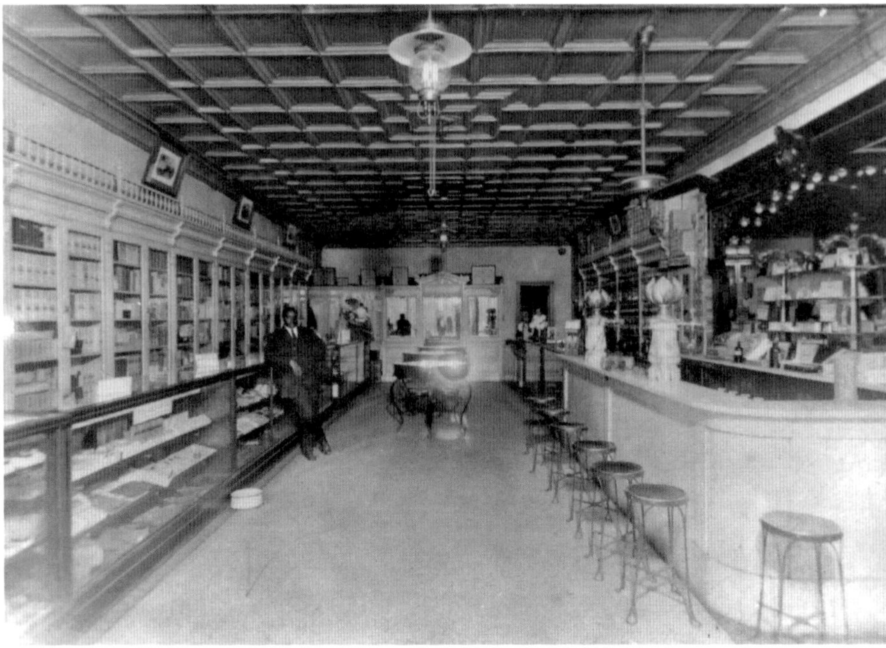

The drugstore where the kids hung out.

the entrance on the left, the sound of a loud machine was quite disturbing. The noise was coming from above the rows of seats. We realized it was the old furnace, so oddly placed in the ceiling above. Because of the sound and vibrations, we did not want to sit directly under it. As we picked our row and sat down, there appeared to be ten or twelve other moviegoers present, all African American.

The movie began, the furnace was putting out heat and all seemed to be well—or so we thought. We became quite comfortable and toasty in the old structure. The banging of the old furnace was still quite menacing, even with the loudness of the movie. As our eyes had adjusted to the darkness, we began to see the others in attendance more clearly. As cold and as icy the weather was outside, the other patrons appeared to be dressed for fall or even spring/summer temperatures. This attire looked rather odd, but we thought nothing of it and returned to the movie. We were distracted shortly thereafter by a commotion at the end of our aisle. A black cat appeared to be chasing a mouse or rat throughout the theater. We had brought with us some snacks and tried to lure the cat to us. My friend caught the cat. It sat with us throughout the rest of the movie.

The movie ended and the lights brightened. As we exited the movie, we noticed the other patrons had already left. Again, we thought this a little strange, since we were sitting toward the back of the movie house. It stands to reason that anyone leaving the facility would have had to pass down the left or right aisle past us. We proceeded to leave the theater and passed the booth with the man still in attendance there. I spoke to him and thanked him for allowing us to see the last movie of the theater's history and said I was sure the other patrons had enjoyed it as well. He looked at me somewhat puzzled and replied, "You boys were the only ones at the 9:00 p.m. showing, and for that matter, there has been no one here all day." Then we realized we were the only live people there and those others were ghosts of old patrons, getting their last look at an old movie palace from long ago, the last picture show.

So we ice-skated our way back home with the black cat under my friend's arm. The theater was razed the next day and the historic African American block and all of its history was gone forever.

Chapter 14

THE OLD DARK HOUSE

You have probably experienced the likes of ghosts, apparitions or just plain scary feelings in old houses over your lifetime. This is the case with many old homes across Winston-Salem.

Our first story takes place in the first suburb of Old Winston, the original West End. In the 1870s and early 1880s, Old Winston was growing immensely. The central downtown has already seen growth after the Civil War with the creation of pocket neighborhoods directly around the downtown of Main Street, Liberty Street, Old Town/Trade Street, Pine/Marshall, Spruce Street and Poplar Street. The early neighborhoods east of Main Street referred to as East Winston had also been created.

Tobacco factories began appearing in the Old Winston landscape in the 1870s. Very quickly, they grew to number in the twenties. When P.H. Hanes and his brother arrived to build their large factory on Chestnut Street, Richard J. Reynolds was not far behind. R.J. Reynolds shortly thereafter bought out the Hanes brothers and consolidated his "Little Red Factory" with theirs. The Hanes brothers changed their profession from tobacco to textiles, and the king of underwear production across the world was born.

Many of the other early tobacco factory owners followed suit in branching out into other professions across the Old Winston landscape. With their windfalls made after being purchased by the R.J. Reynolds tobacco company, these men and their families created the first suburb of Old Winston, the wealthy West End. The original West End of these former tobacco magnates—bordered by West Fourth Street, North Broad Street,

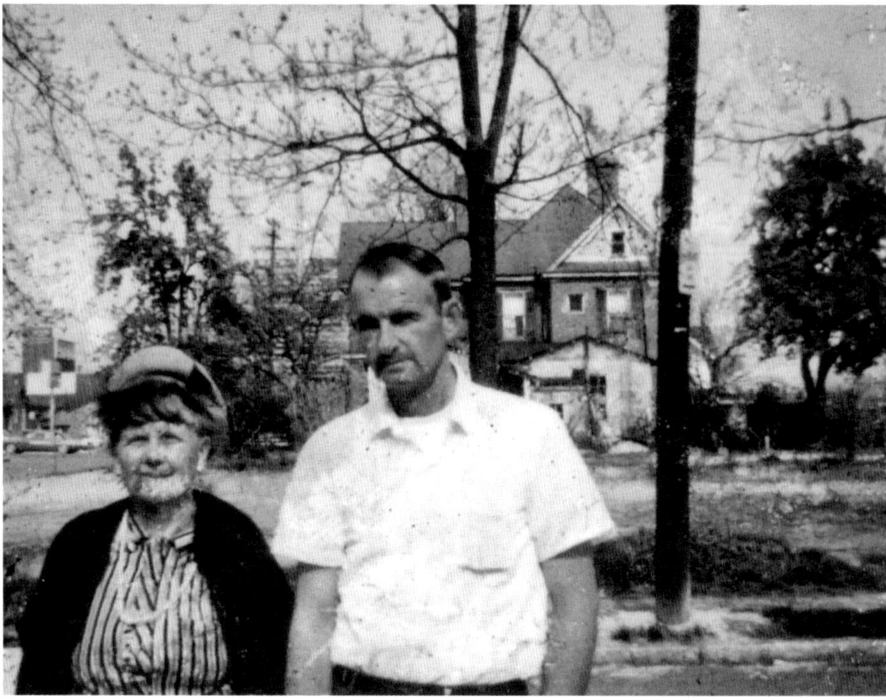

Grandmother Mary and Uncle Don with the "Old Dark House," the Efird mansion, in the background, circa 1967.

North Green Street and Brookstown Avenue—included the Winston Graded School circa 1882. The school was the first in Winston-Salem created by educator and state superintendent Calvin Wiley. Mr. Wiley almost single-handedly rebuilt the education system of North Carolina after the Civil War. He founded the graded school system concept that was used throughout most of the twentieth century.

The Efrid family mansion was a circa 1880 three-story Victorian brownstone and brick structure in the heart of the Old West End. Mr. Efrid, the patriarch of the family, sold his tobacco interest early on, and the family moved into the grocery and mercantile business. Their early department store, Efird's, was a prominent clothing store on West Fourth Street for many years. The Efirds also had a grocery and sundry shop on North Main Street near the Court House Square.

I had the opportunity to meet Mr. Efrid in the late 1960s. His home at the corner of North Broad Street and Holly Avenue composed the complete 200 block of Broad, Holly and Green Street, with a street on its east side, its north side and its west side. My grandmother's home was directly one block west at 228 North Green Street. The home was a two-story Victorian wood-frame structure, circa 1880. This type of home plan was the choice of many less prominent tobacco men, but it was a nineteenth-century mansion nonetheless.

The Efrid home was empty throughout the 1960s and 1970s. Mr. Efrid, well into his eighties, came weekly to check on the property and collect parking revenue money from city employees who parked there. Since the back lot of the homeplace sat directly across the street from my grandmother's house, it was easy to observe the house throughout the day and night. Mr. Efrid often visited my grandmother to reminisce about old times since she and his deceased wife had been good friends over the years. During one of the visits, I was sitting with my grandmother on the front porch, and I had the opportunity to ask Mr. Efrid why no one resided in his family's homeplace. Specifically, I did not ever recall him going into the old structure.

Mr. Efrid was usually straightforward with most questions asked of him, and his response to this one was no different. He replied, "The house gives me the creeps. I know this is the homeplace of my birth, but ever since my wife passed and brothers and sisters are deceased, a cold feeling overcame me the last times I was there." He went on to tell me that it had been more than three years since he had set foot into the old mansion. My grandmother and I related to Mr. Efrid our observations of the house after dark. He was flabbergasted to hear of the lights that roamed through the house, usually between 10:00 p.m. to 11:00 p.m., nearly every night. My grandmother reported that she believed the light resembled the glow from an old kerosene lamp. Mr. Efrid became somewhat pale, almost as white as a ghost, as he relayed how every evening after everyone was in bed, his young wife used to check on the family with a lantern in tow. He thought this could have been the spirit of his deceased wife haunting the old dark house.

I told Mr. Efrid and my grandmother that we needed to go ghost hunting. I was reminded of the spooky stories from my early days at the old Green Front Cash Store. I said that we needed to find out the answers to this haunting question. They both laughed and asked if I was kidding. An emphatic no was my answer. My grandmother's demeanor became serious, and she looked at Mr. Efrid for his response. Both answered in unison with excited gleams in their eyes, "Yes!"

Mr. Efrid returned about 9:30 p.m. Mr. Efrid, my grandmother Mary and I ventured across the street to the field behind the old spooky mansion. The closer we came to the house, the more suspenseful the situation became.

The house was huge. Mr. Efrid and my grandmother began to feel more apprehensive the closer we got. We circled the home twice and found no one in sight. All businesses and homes in the area were dark as well. My watch read 10:00 p.m. when we walked back toward the field to get a better view of the old house. What happened next sent chills up and down our spines.

A light appeared in the second-story window and appeared to move throughout the home, passing by the many windows that covered the house. Then it disappeared for a moment, only to reappear in the third-story window. Mr. Efrid spoke first: "That's the ghost of my wife!" He said when she was alive, she made took same route through the home fifty or sixty years ago on her nightly path. He also added that she would venture to the ground floor and check the locks on downstairs doors and windows next.

With that information, I bolted toward the house's nearest window for a closer view. As I peered into the window, my jaw dropped. A young lady in a flowing nightdress of white entered the room, continuing by the window of my view. Mr. Efrid and my grandmother were one step ahead of me. While I was mesmerized by the lady in the glow of the lantern as she literally glided across the floor, they entered the back door of the room that held the apparition. The scene played out in a surrealistic way that seemed more dream than reality. The spiritual ghost lady and the solid living human beings, Mr. Efrid and my grandmother, contrasted as starkly as night and day. The light of the ghost lantern added to this haunting episode, but what happened next changed everything for those involved at the old dark house. The spirit lady was instantly identified by Mr. Efrid and my grandmother as they called the lady's name. The ghost seemed to stop in midair and hover. I saw smiles come upon all three faces within the room.

What I witnessed next makes me still question my sanity, even today. The spirit of Mr. Efrid's dearly departed wife moved quietly and surrounded my grandmother's body. With her body draped in an aura of beautiful white light, my grandmother gave Mr. Efrid a hug that lasted for several minutes. I raced to enter the house, fearing for my grandmother's life. As I entered, the whole room was filled with a calm, warm atmosphere, almost heavenly. The aura dispersed, and the room returned to its nightly darkness. Mr. Efrid and my grandmother discontinued the hug and looked at each other, puzzled.

We left the home and returned to my grandmother's house. We discussed for over an hour what we had experienced at the old dark house.

Mr. Efrid believed his wife's spirit had waited for him to reenter the home these many years. The abandonment of the homeplace created a void in the house, and his return brought back the homey feeling that had existed there since the 1880s. My grandmother felt the presence of Mrs. Efrid in the aura that overwhelmed her. For those few minutes, Mrs. Efrid was able to reconnect with Mr. Efrid through my grandmother.

Over the next year, Mr. Efrid fixed up the home and sold it to a family just starting out. Mr. Efrid passed away not long after his old homestead was sold, and my grandmother and family moved away from 228 North Green Street not long thereafter. Unfortunately, my grandmother's home on Green Street across from Mr. Efrid's mansion did not have a happy ending. A historical preservationist's nightmare had arrived on the horizon of the neighborhood: urban renewal.

OUR NEXT TALE IS SPUN from the inner city neglect of Winston-Salem. Many of the houses in and around downtown Winston-Salem of the 1960s and early 1970s were still owned by the original families who had helped create the wealth and growth of the town in the late nineteenth and early twentieth centuries. A few larger mansions in Old West End had been converted into rental properties during the Great Depression and War World II. They were known as apartment houses, and the dwellings had been sectioned off so several families could live in one homestead during these lean years. During the 1950s and 1960s, these apartment houses were used extensively with the advent of the baby boomer generation, of which I was a part. Today, the apartment houses are called condominiums.

By the late 1960s, the old mansions had seen their better days, and historic preservation was little help since the historic movement was in its infancy across the United States. Old Salem's preservation movement began in 1950, but it was confined to the neighborhood of Old Salem alone. Historic preservation beyond Old Salem arrived in 1978, nearly thirty years later, with the second historic district, West End. Unfortunately, this was not the original West End neighborhood that contained the Winston graded school site and the old tobacco magnates' mansions along Broad Street and Green Street—or what was left of them.

The federal program of urban renewal had arrived to the streets of Winston-Salem in the late 1960s. The gist of the program was to clean up inner-city slums and replace rundown buildings with modern ones and new development. Local historians who wanted to preserve Old Winston history coined the phrase that described the federal program as "urban removal." The workings of historic preservation were not included in urban renewal. The old-timers, along with many others, believed an old expression applied perfectly for urban renewal's snub of historic preservation: simply put, "they threw the baby out with the bathwater."

Before the wrecking ball found its way to these old mansions, several had tales to tell. The Efrid homeplace was our first. The second was an even larger mansion at the corner of North Broad Street and Brookstown Avenue. The mansion was built in the 1890s, and as the owner aged, he became more eccentric and more of what the old-timers called "an old cuss." He did not believe in banks and decided to bury his money throughout his mansion. The basement, walls, the attic and more became his bank vault. But when the old mansion was singled out, due to urban renewal, to have its day with the wrecking ball, it seemed the recently deceased owner had other plans for his property.

Rite Construction Demolition Company had contracted the rights to demolish many houses in the 1950s and 1960s in Salem and Winston. The company would long remember this one. The preparation to demolish the house was no different from any other except for one important factor—this house refused to die. The old-timers had heard the demolition started off slow since most of the home was to be salvaged. It was thought with this house that if it met the wrecking ball and salvaging could be done on a slower process, some hidden fortune might be revealed in the old dark house. The salvagers worked on one room at a time, gutting out the walls meticulously, hoping treasures could be found.

However, the wreckers could not believe what they experienced. The smell of the old deceased owner's cigar and his apparition periodically appeared to the workers. Several quit their jobs entirely because they feared what evil could be in the house—but that was not the half of it. When the salvagers/treasure hunters returned the next day to start on another room of the haunted home, the previous room—plaster walls and all—had been reconstructed. Mr. Johns was an eyewitness to this reconstructive work. He stated, "I still do not believe what I saw. The room that I had seen the previous day, gutted, was as if nothing had been done to it the next day." The house was eventually demolished. When asked by residents of the neighborhood weeks later about the strange occurrences of re-creation or if a treasure had been found, the wrecking crew said only, "No comment." Mr. Johns concluded, "The wrecking company closed for awhile and reportedly took a long, needed vacation after their experience in the old dark house."

Chapter 15

The Devil Will Get You if You Don't Watch Out

Our next tale of haunted history was relayed with solemn, unadulterated respect by the old-timers on a cold, dark night, supposedly on the anniversary of the death of the woman who had lived only a stone's throw away from the Green Front Cash Store, the store we occupied that night. It had been thirty years ago to the day in the heart of the Great Depression when this tale ended in death. The beginning of our story occurred on October 10, 1929, a few weeks before Halloween and the stock market crash that began the Great Depression.

"I would like to say the woman was well thought of, a family lady with children and a husband who loved her, but I cannot," said Mr. Johns. "She was detested by her family, who wanted nothing to do with her. Her family had abandoned the woman, and her co-workers at the mill were just plain terrified of her."

My grandmother, a Christian lady who found good in everyone, had known the woman and defined her simply as wicked. Several of the old-timers expressed the feelings of the neighborhood in which she lived when they reported that she was the most selfish, self-centered, God-hating person who ever lived. The quiet one needed to know, and I just had to ask: "How could anyone be so reviled by everyone?"

"Oh," Mr. Johns spoke up. "She had someone for whom she had sacrificed her family, one who loved her immensely—the devil, Satan himself." I asked if she had feelings for the devil as well. Everyone chuckled at my response and question. Mr. Johns chimed in, "Michael, she did not believe in the devil

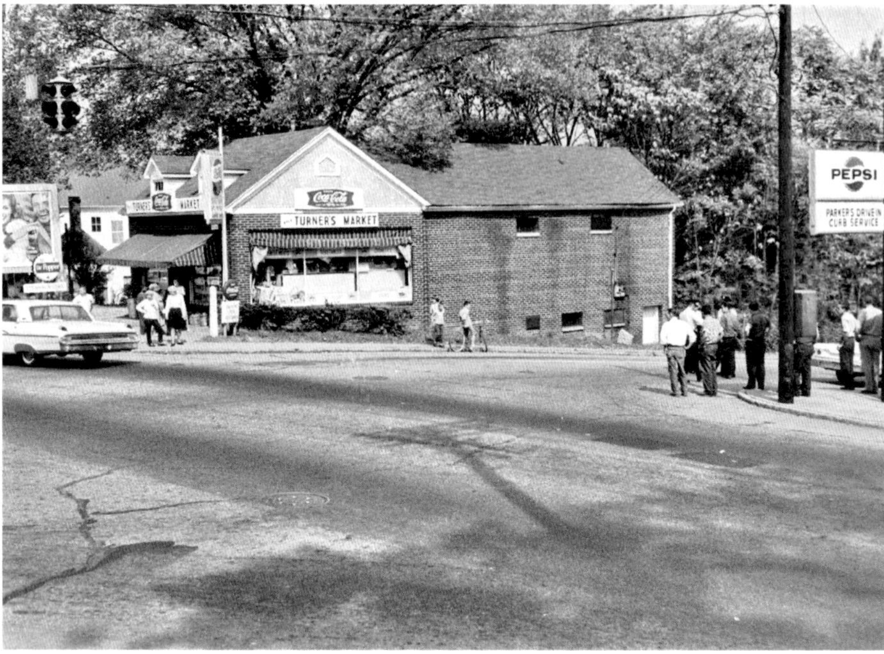

The Green Front Cash Store at the crossroads of Winston and Salem.

or God. She was an atheist, but not a person who claimed to be an atheist because they did not believe in organized religion—Christianity and the like. She was one who believed in no one but herself. Scientifically, if she could have been any structure in the solar system, it would have been the sun so everything in the system would revolve around her."

It was reported that when any church group or individual of charitable interests approached the woman during the Depression years to solicit help for the church or the downtrodden, she simply began to laugh so satanically that, if there were children close by, they would break down in fits of uncontrollable crying.

The woman had a good childhood. Her mother and father provided well for her and her sister. When the lady married and had children, everything changed, almost overnight. She and her family had just moved to Winston after her husband was transferred from another city in North Carolina. They rented a small house on North Green Street in the Old West End of the 1910s. The woman had a good inheritance, and her husband had gotten a promotion from his transfer. She was even able to volunteer at the local hospital, the Twin City Hospital, which was literally around the corner from her. In an earlier

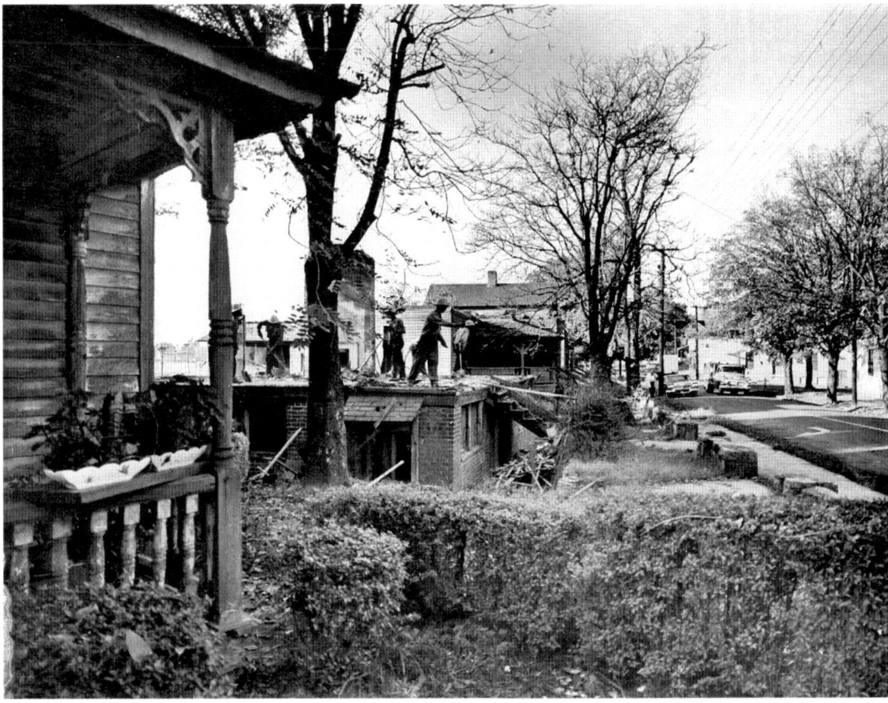

Mama Brietz's cotton field, circa 1914. The land of the pre–Civil War cotton field was originally part of the Paper Mill Settlement.

tale, our readers were introduced to the problems associated with the hospital, and it appeared to have an effect on the woman of this tale as well.

She worked a couple days a week as a volunteer for the Annie Grogan charitable group that had created the Twin City Hospital and later founded the City Hospital in 1914. The woman had always been attracted to charitable groups, like the Grogan one, and she hoped her services would expand even further in charitable ways if she could be noticed by the charitable organizations. She was noticed all right—but not in the way she had intended.

Her first encounter with evil—real evil—occurred on a short lunch on the grounds of the hospital near the infamous graveyard of the haunted block tale. It was a beautiful, sunny day, and the woman wanted to take advantage and have a short, quiet, private picnic on the hospital grounds. As she sat on a small blanket that she had borrowed, she ate her lunch, which tasted delicious. However, in this landscape, as has been reported in a previous tale and will be reported in future tales, what lies beneath in the boughs of

Old Winston can be very dangerous. As she sat and finished her lunch, the graveyard site seemed to draw her to it. She had a few minutes before she was due back to the hospital, so she strolled through the maze of graves there. She noticed that many graves had no names, just plain markers. The woman felt remorse for the unknown souls buried here in this unkempt place and vowed to return and clean it up. The next day, she was back with broom and brush in hand to do just that.

She had barely gotten started cleaning a headstone when a voice seemed to radiate from the ground at this grave site. She also noticed that the grave had sunken down several inches into the ground and small holes were visible around it. The sounds became more distinct as she squatted down toward the holes. The sounds appeared to be voices from beyond the grave. A chill went up her spine. She gained her composure while pushing her fear aside. The woman listened intently to better understand the words. Shock overcame her when she realized the words were her name and the calls were for help.

She returned to the hospital, found a mid-sized shovel and returned to the grave site and proceeded to dig it up. The desecration of the grave began the woman on a course spiraling downward. Her demeanor changed overnight after the incident, to the point where her family thought she was possessed by evil. They did not realize how close to the truth they were. The woman's actions, as reported by her co-workers and the locals in the neighborhood, were her first encounter with insanity. Her volunteer days were over.

She became so greedy with her inheritance and her husband's income that she refused to pay the bills or even buy food. Unfortunately, the family's relationship was destroyed, and her husband and children could no longer be around her. They left her and the city behind. As the woman grew older through the 1920s, her disposition and situation became darker. She squandered her inheritance, and most people who were exposed to her at the small house she rented on Green Street for more than ten years simply referred to her as "the witch."

Two weeks before Halloween and the stock market crash of 1929, the woman was working in her yard, cleaning up the autumn leaves that covered the lawn. The whole time she worked, she cursed like sailor at the beautiful leaves that had fallen and the wind as it blew the leaves—even the sunset did not escape her scorn. The families who lived close to the woman often made sure their children were inside when she was working outside, for obvious reasons.

The woman had realized the sun had almost set and all the neighbors had returned to their homes. It was quiet, and she was alone, just the way

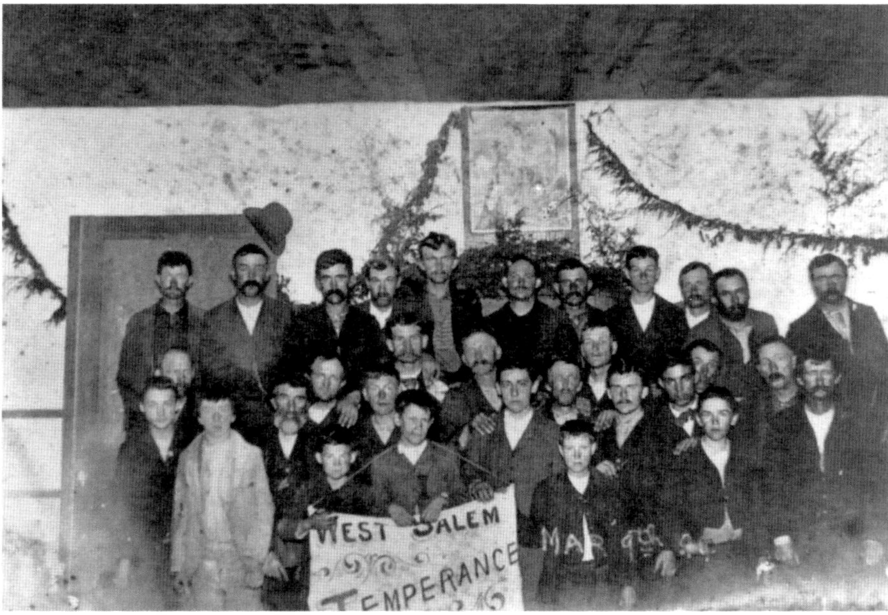

The West Salem Temperance Society (circa 1890s) was instrumental in fighting the evils of alcohol and the evils of the supernatural.

she liked it. This evening was different, and what came next would change her life forever. The woman had the feeling someone was watching her. She believed it was a nosy neighbor, as she called most of them, and thought to herself that she would have some fun—evil fun, at that. She reportedly cackled and said to the entity behind her, "I know you are back there, you scared, lazy piece of trash. Come out here where I can see you, and I will hurt you real bad." The sunset cast the shadow of the entity in front of her. She screamed when the outline of the shadow revealed a tall man with horns. As she turned to face her watcher, a curse word on her lips, the woman immediately became frozen with fear as the entity spoke: "I know you do not believe in me, but I believe in you, and in two weeks, on Halloween night, I will return to claim what is mine—you!"

The woman passed out as the last word was spoken and did not awake until the next morning with the arrival of the egg man. She had two weeks until the dark one would return. The locals, including Mr. Johns, believed at that exact moment of the woman's encounter with her lost love, the atheist belief she had held so close had departed her post haste. Amazingly, in less than two weeks, she became the most religious, kind and thoughtful person in Winston-Salem. She told all who would listen of her plight with the devil. When the fateful day, Halloween, arrived, she took her new Bible and returned to the front yard where her visitor had first arrived. The woman remained there until sunset. The shadow and the entity returned at its stated time, and the woman proceeded to beg and plead for her life without him, while the devil just snickered and spoke these words: "You were mine from the beginning, and you will be mine for all eternity. So leave this human and her body and come—now!'

The woman awoke two days later in the City Hospital after the horror had left her and returned to God knows where. She responded to the doctors and nurses that a burden had been lifted off her shoulders and she belonged to God now. It was reported by Mr. Johns that the woman joined the Catholic faith and the nunnery not long after. This woman had come full circle in life; the evil that had possessed her was gone. I have always believed this lady's identity and name should not be used, and I hope our readers understand why. The evil that appeared that day at the old hospital graveyard in this tale and others could return, darker and more determined to possess another. So just to be on the safe side, always remember: on those cool October nights around the old neighborhoods of the city, be careful, or the devil may get you if you don't watch out.

Chapter 16

Westdale and the Wall to Nowhere

The Old Shallowford Road, the first road into Salem circa 1765, has seen much history develop around it over the years. Sections of the old road evolved into the old streets of Winston-Salem, such as North Street (First Street) and Old Shallowford Road (Broad Street and Academy Street), to name a couple. Branch-type streets forked off the Old Shallowford Road and created their own local history and haunted history as well. One such branch street, known as Westdale Avenue in current times, is the site of our next tale.

Research does not reveal the early names of Westdale Avenue. Most local residents believed the streets were paved and the sidewalks cut in the 1920s, so this was most likely when the name originated. Throughout the downtown, many older structures were added on to through updates and modernization. One such update period was 1900. The new century was dawning, and everyone in Winston and Salem had modernization fever. City and real estate leaders advertised this theme during the Roaring Twenties: "No one need live in an outdated home, update now and your home will be considered to be a new and modern home on the tax records and real-estate listings." This was fine and good for raising taxes and selling houses, but it created a difficulty for local historians as far as honest and truthful dating of older structures over the years.

This was the case for our tale's main character, the Westdale Wall. Currently, if one travels down the short street of Westdale Avenue, one will find a dead-end street, a large hill and a small stream that dead-ends itself into a culvert. Nothing unusual about that scene—except when one looks to the left before arriving to the dead end, where a very old and well-constructed rock wall can be found. Old-timers said the wall used to connect and extend nearly to First Street (Old Shallowford Road).

Mr. Johns, who had shared much history with the author of the Paper Mill Settlement, the area along Peters Creek and the parkway today, explained, "The ridge to the north of the Paper Mill Settlement and beyond the ridge that housed the Caves of West Salem became a part of the Paper Mill Rock Quarry development." In today's landscape, this area began where Peters Creek Parkway bridge passes over Business Interstate 40, northward to First Street. Westdale Avenue sat at the bottom of the ridge and Peters Creek Parkway at the top of the ridge. Mr. Johns continued: "The rock quarry of the Paper Mill Settlement wanted to expand from its original location." The original location of the first rock quarry in today's landscape was on the east side of Peters Creek Parkway, below the ridge of the Old West Salem caves between the on-ramp of Business 40 and Bank Street. Mr. Johns stated, "The expansion of the rock quarry took place between 1805 and 1810 along the ridge at the future Westdale Avenue site at Apple Street Stream." Apple Street Stream, before the arrival of Peters Creek Parkway and Business 40, continued to the original rock quarry site.

The rock ridge along Westdale Avenue peaks in the backyards of residents on Park Circle. The Park Circle neighborhood was part of a pocket neighborhood that circled off First Street and looped back just to the east of its beginning. The circular neighborhood was an experiment in 1918 at the end of World War I by city planners to design a street with a park area in the middle. Mr. Johns believed this was an idea drawn from the history of the Paper Mill Settlement to commemorate and recognize the "Great Expansion of 1805 to 1815," when thousands of wagon trains came through the area. The concept of the wagon wheel was the blueprint for the street.

The backyards of the Park Circle residents held clues and remnants of the quarry behind several houses, where large exposed-granite boulders and shavings of the long-lost quarry site were found. From the location of the wall, it was most likely constructed from rocks of the Paper Mill Quarry. Westdale Avenue was paved and sidewalked over the original quarry road. This was a dirt path that was connected to the original quarry with this new addition. Mr. Johns explained, "There were three farms/plantations. One to the northwest, the Fries (circa 1800), and to the southeast, the Brietz (circa 1838) and the Leinbach (circa 1820). These farm borders made up the Paper Mill Settlement, including the rock quarry."

A friend of my grandmother's resided at Park Circle in one of the houses that had remnants of the rock quarry in the backyard. During the 1940s, the lady of the house had some health problems and needed a nurse and a maid for several years. Both the nurse and maid related their own stories surrounding this area of our tale. I interviewed the son of the resident in the 1970s. The son and his mother were present when these two tales were told.

The nurse had been practicing her profession for nearly forty years at local hospitals, including the North Carolina Baptist, presently Wake Forest Bowman Gray, and the City Hospital, now closed. In the 1940s, she was doing in-home care. When the nurse began her profession in the early 1900s, she had just finished training at the Twin City Hospital. She was not married and lived literally behind the hospital in the old mansion on the Plank Road now called Westdale Avenue. The son at the Park Circle home had friends on Westdale, and the wall had fascinated them for many years. They coined the name, the Wall to Nowhere. The nurse detailed to the son how the mansion was a wood-frame, three-story structure and extended halfway up the old Plank Road. She stated the homeplace was pre–Civil War and had a front porch that extended the complete length of the house. She lived there with other nurses and single ladies who were entering the workforce. She was told the large house had been used as a hotel of sorts for all the workers and guests who came to the area over many years during the expansion of the Paper Mill Settlement. She believed the old rambling mansion to be haunted. She was scared to stay at night and was so glad when she found an apartment near the hospital on Brookstown Avenue. Before she moved, she reported hearing rocking chairs often late at night, many of them in unison rocking back and forth on the long front porch. When she went to see to the commotion, no people or chairs were to be found. Chattering and banjo playing was heard throughout the night, especially on the weekends. Again, no one was to be seen, and it would become as quiet as a mouse when she went to investigate.

The nurse was asked how she got around the area. She reported that a dirt path led from the side of the mansion up the ridge and turned to intersect with old Shallowford Road, First Street today. She remembered when the new roads and sidewalk projects began in 1919 during the modernization of the city. The old mansion was torn down, like many of the old buildings from the antebellum time period. She said she did not miss the old mansion since her memories of all the frightful actions in this haunted structure left her in despair. She returned to the street in the mid-1920s and admired the beautiful homes being built there. As she returned to the site of the old

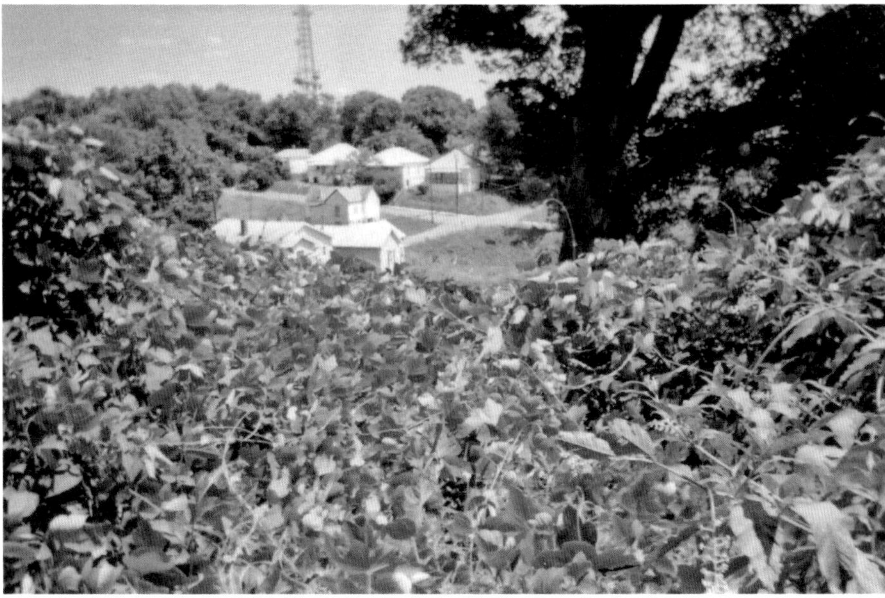

The hidden valley of the Watkins Street neighborhood before the homes were razed for the BB&T Ballfield complex. Photo circa 2012.

haunted mansion, only the rock wall was there to greet her—and she was mighty glad for that.

The maid's tale was one of sadness and horror. Her mother had been a child during the Civil War and lived in the Watkins Street neighborhood, located near the Park Circle neighborhood. The maid relayed, "My mother was a little girl during the Civil War, and my grandparents were slaves at the Fries plantation just west of here. Many of her family members were brought to the quarry site to work. I was allowed to visit older family members, who gained their freedom and had moved to the area between the plantation of Mr. Fries and Mr. Brietz. When the war ended, chaos was everywhere for my people throughout the area. Many had no jobs except those as slaves, which were now gone. The first winter at the end of the Civil War was horrible. My grandparents told my mother that many of her relatives, former slaves, had frozen to death that cold, harsh winter."

The lady described how she had grown up and moved to the Watkins Street neighborhood, where she still resided. She said the neighborhood had many memories, good and bad. Many generations of family members before and after the Civil War had lived all their lives between the borders of Broad Street, Brookstown Avenue, Peters Creek and Bank Street. She said, "My grandfather had worked on plantations and had worked at old rock quarry behind the very house where we sit today on Park Circle. He told stories of a large hotel there that was as busy with people coming and going as those hotels in Winston around the Courthouse Square. My mother told me this old place was torn down after 1900. She believed the place had seen bad things happen over the years and the place had many haints in it."

Westdale Avenue has evolved over these many years. The Watkins and Park Circle neighborhoods have disappeared into history, with only a few houses remaining. The haunting and the deaths surrounding them are remembered today only at Westdale and the Wall to No Where.

Chapter 17

The House That Moved

The Old West End, the first suburb of Winston, had seen its better days by 1970. The oldest part of the West End had been ravaged by urban renewal, the blight of the older neighborhood and the reluctance to acknowledge the rich history of the town beyond the 1950 Historic District of Old Salem. The tale presented with this chapter appears to have its creation in the culmination of all the negative energy attached to the older homes, businesses and mansions of Old Winston-Salem. "Throwing the baby out with the bathwater" could have been the epitaph of the old structures; however, an event occurred that could have changed things or at least drawn attention to the blight of our architectural treasures and their history, which had been downplayed and proverbially swept under the rug by city and government leaders.

Our tale takes place on North Green Street at the corner of Second Street. Today, an empty lot is all that is left of the house that moved. The landscape surrounding the house had been a hotbed of supernatural activity for years. The old dark house and the haunted block existed one block east and one block west, respectively, of North Green Street, which was originally called Pond Street. The old-timers reported that Pond Street was chosen as the official name of the street when the Winston Graded School and the first suburb of Winston were created in the 1880s. Long before the town of Winston was born, one of many underground streams snaked throughout this part of Old West Salem. When the stream rose to the surface, a pond was formed. Mr. Johns stated, "The area of North Green Street, North

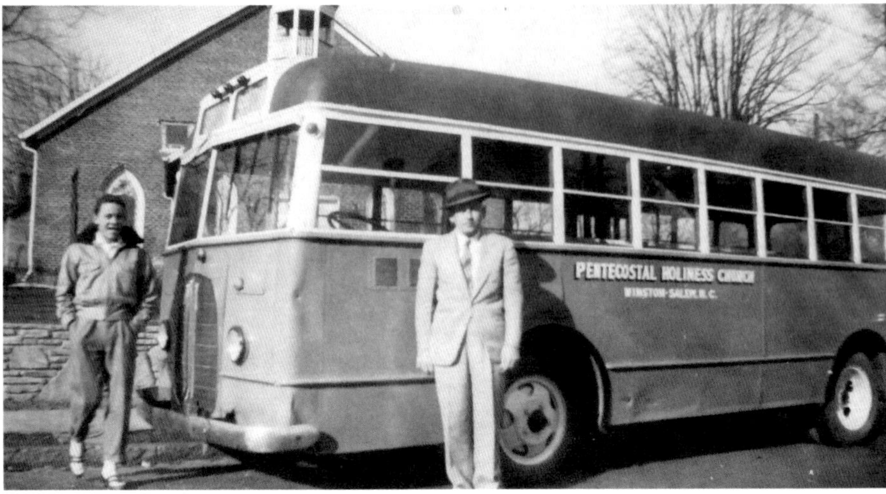

Henry Ruark knew the man whose house exploded.

Broad Street and West Fourth Street were part of a rock plateau nearly one thousand feet above sea level. After Salem was founded, the resources of the pond, including the abundant hardwood trees, were cherished by the Moravians." Since the pond was naturally formed, Mother Nature had made it possible to channel water to the east, west, north and south of the future town. Mr. Johns stated, "The pond simply dried up shortly before the Civil War. The streams continued underground, but the locals always felt a dark force had destroyed the beautiful green space that many families once picnicked at while their children swam in the pond."

A dark force had been prevalent throughout this section of Old West Salem and later West End over the years. President Washington had experienced a dark, supernatural event; the had shaman felt the force at the Paper Mill Settlement even before his journey to rid the curse from the Fansler Farm, and the lost graveyard of paranormal activity at the Twin City Hospital had to be dealt with as well. Between 1968 and 1973, as urban renewal claimed one historic structure after another, the "Halloween Houses," as the teenagers in the neighborhood of West Salem and West End called them, were created from several old mansions. During a five-year period, the haunted house concept was played out within these mansions.

Several local organizations contributed to the new trends during October across downtown Winston-Salem. The Junior League, the School of the Arts and several other clubs brought horror and the supernatural, even though the scary Halloween scenes were created with makeup and special

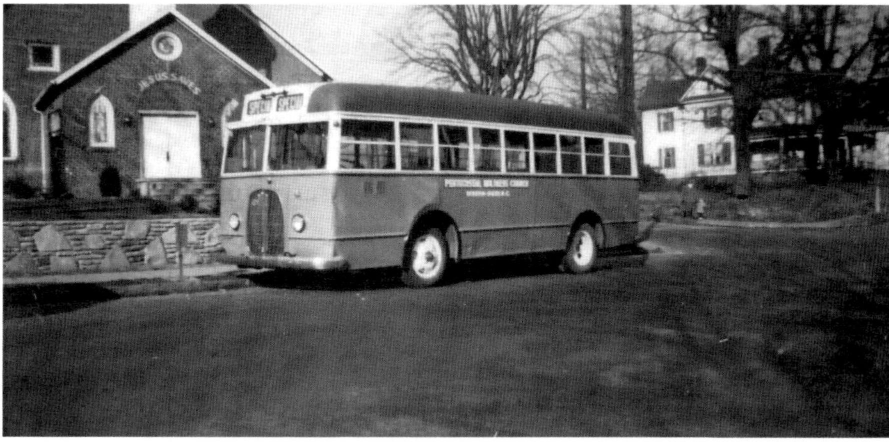

The Pentecostal Holiness Church and church bus corner of North Broad Street and Brookstown Avenue. The Old Dark House, a mansion of another tobacco magnate, was to the right of church.

effects. October had always been a time of festivals, fairs and, of course, the Halloween season of the witch. My favorite time of the year is October and the autumn season, and those five years of haunted houses rekindled those late nights at the Green Front Cash Store.

I could have never imagined the effect the haunted houses along Broad Street had on the central character of our story, the house that moved. I had the opportunity to speak with the creators of the special effects of the haunted houses along Broad Street. The creators claimed the special effects and the makeup was just the background to the horror and fear of this performance. The real fear was created not artificially but by real paranormal activity occurring throughout the houses during the Halloween shows. As the creator explained in more detail, the old rundown mansions seemed to take on lives of their own. Lights, shadows and sounds were experienced and a demonic creature was even seen in the old house at the corner of Broad and Second Streets. The house was located one block east and directly across from the house of our tale. The demon creature, which was not part of the special effects, reportedly spoke in a deep, gutteral voice to those in the rooms it walked by.

The creator of the special effects spoke with animosity when he said the creature scared him and all who had seen and heard it nearly to death. Several of the participants fainted, and others needed medical assistance. The creature reportedly said, "You people have destroyed my desecrated places for the last time, now it's your time." The creature disappeared in one of the best

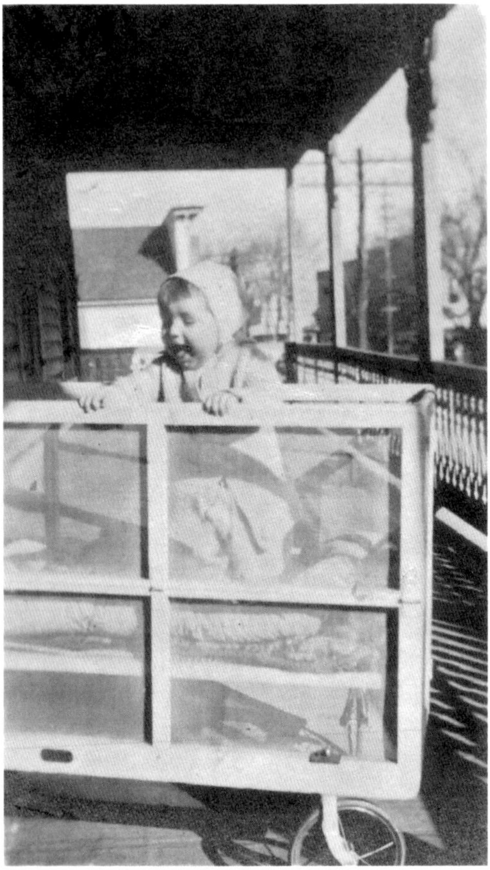

Little Raymond Brietz on the porch of the Brietz homestead beside the West Salem Fire Station on South Green at Apple Streets. Photo circa 1914.

disappearing acts the creator of the special effects said that he would ever hope to see. The creator said he knew every person on his staff personally, and this creature was not one of them.

Within days after this Halloween became history, the wrecking ball claimed another victim: the creature's homeplace.

The first week of November arrived with a chill in the air on North Green Street. This was odd because the temperature read seventy-nine degrees. Then the most unexpected event happened. The home on North Green Street at the corner of Second Street exploded—literally. The house was blown on its side, and the roof lay upside down beside the collapsed homeplace. The family was not at home, and the house was empty. The city and the fire department reported that the accident was the result of a gas leak, but the owners claimed the gas had not been turned on since the previous winter. Many residents in the area had heard the prediction of the so-called creature and its description of what would happen if its homeplace were destroyed. Well, the mansion where the creature had been seen had been razed.

The city officials, the insurance company and the owners of the house did not have any more discussion of the issues concerning any of the events over the past week. Unfortunately, this evil had not been appeased and returns in our final tale.

Chapter 18

The Chanting Monks

"WHOOOO Halloween's Coming" became a catchphrase in the late 1950s and into the 1960s. Every year at this time, the leaves change, the air becomes brisk, autumn is well underway and the things that go bump in the night are upon us. This was the meaning of Halloween to the baby boomer generation, of which I was a part. The papers read like this in the 1950s and 1960s during Halloween: "Witches and goblins will ride Friday night in the city recreation department's salute to one of the oldest festivals in the world." Halloween had its beginning in the time of the Druids and has various titles ranging from All Saints Eve and All Hallows Eve to Nutcrack Night and Snapapple Night.

Neighborhood parades could be found in the evenings around Halloween at Hanes Baseball Park, Miller Park Amphitheatre, Granville School, Cardinal Baseball Park, Forest Park Baseball Field, Hanes High School, Kimberly Park, Atkins High School baseball diamond, Columbia Heights and Happy Hill, to name a few. Parades were divided into individuals, couples and groups. The marchers progressed, and if you were tapped on the shoulder by the judges, you continued to the final grand finale. Teenagers' Halloween fun was found at dances sponsored by the Winston-Salem Public Schools. The dances were held at Reynolds Gymnasium, Miller Park, Granville Teenage Clubroom, Gray High School and Hanes High School. Even Old Salem's own Salem College joined the festivities with a day of witches and damsels in distress paraded throughout the campus.

Halloween's two chief characteristics in ancient days were the lighting of the bonfires and the belief that this is the night in the year during which ghosts and witches are most likely to wander abroad. History shows that the main celebrations of Halloween were purely Druid in nature. Ireland appears partly responsible for the "treat or trick" idea of today. In Scotland, cabbage or kale used to be a highlight of Halloween celebrations, with kale broth or cabbage broth being an inseparable part of the feast. In both old Ireland and Scotland, a dish named "Call-Cannon" was served. It consisted of mashed parsnips, potatoes and chopped onions, into which was dropped a gold ring. The mixture was put in a large bowl, hollowed in the center and filled with melted butter. When the guests were served, the couple who found the ring was sure to be married within the year. If already married, the finder would be followed by good luck throughout the year.

As the baby boomers enjoyed their parties, dances and the like during the Halloweens of my youth, most of the populace was not aware of what the dark side of All Hallows Eve could bring to our town. More than two hundred years ago, a band of Druids from ancient Europe arrived to America and found their way to North Carolina's "Grand Central Station," the Paper Mill Settlement. Early on after arriving to the hamlet of Salem, they settled into the caves of West Salem. The Druids appeared to have evolved and adapted to our American culture. The Druids were described as heathens in the Protestant religion, but locally they became known as the "Chanting Monks."

In Europe, the Druids of ancient times kept in the shadows and worshipped earth and nature in their own form of religion. Locally, the monks also enjoyed privacy but not in the shadows. The tunnels and mines born from the gold, copper and mineral mines of the gold rush of Old Winston intersected with the caves of Old West Salem. The old-timers said that the monks were very adaptable and what some called magic. They were able to traverse underground in ways even the seasoned miners could not explain.

Wells and well houses were found throughout Old Winston and Old West Salem landscape. An old wives' tale that has been around since Winston-Salem's early days says that if a person visits a neighbor's well, a dead loved one can be communicated with through the underground streams. The old-timers believed the communication was instigated by the monks from the underground tunnels, which were adjacent to the underground streams that fueled the many wells located in the town. Mr. Johns reported: "The wells that were said to have these voices of the chanting monks begin to grow darker. The voices, as well as the chanting, was at first soothing and dreamlike to those who had lost loved ones; however, the voices turned brash, and the dreamlike state turned into a nightmare. The voice began to instruct those who listened to literally turn on their neighbors. Gossip and heinous accusations against their fellow man and woman were encouraged, which frightened and puzzled the people. Those involved were even ashamed to contact the authorities because the voice said they would only be ridiculed and put down by their leaders. The residents contacted the old miners and proceeded to the old mine sites and the caves of Old West Salem. They were determined to find these monks and end the nightmare."

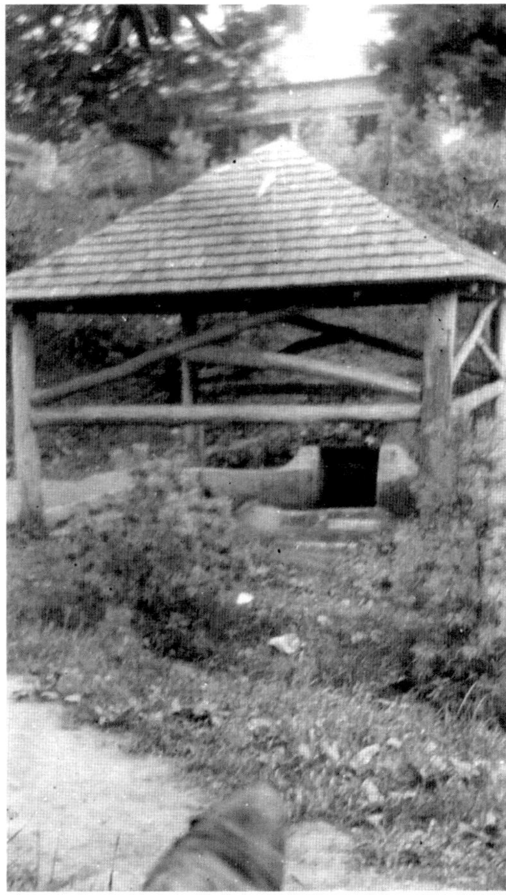

The Kreuser-Brietz well house that was similar to many well houses located in Winston and Salem.

The old miners knew their way around the underbelly of Old Winston, and they found the Druids' hideout. It seemed over the years the monks had been digging their own tunnels to connect to the other ones and to the caves. There was an elaborate system of wooden pipes in a large cavern underground that the monks had discovered. The cavern was decorated with strange symbols and crude pictures of creatures or beings, primitive and grotesque. After studying the situation, those in attendance believed something evil had taken over the Druids and possibly had destroyed them. The old miners told the others that this was an abomination to God and must be destroyed. The miners agreed to eradicate the cavern. The workers left, and the old miners destroyed the cavern. There was nothing said by the townspeople or by the old-timers about this incident. Law enforcement and the city leaders were never notified. The fate of the

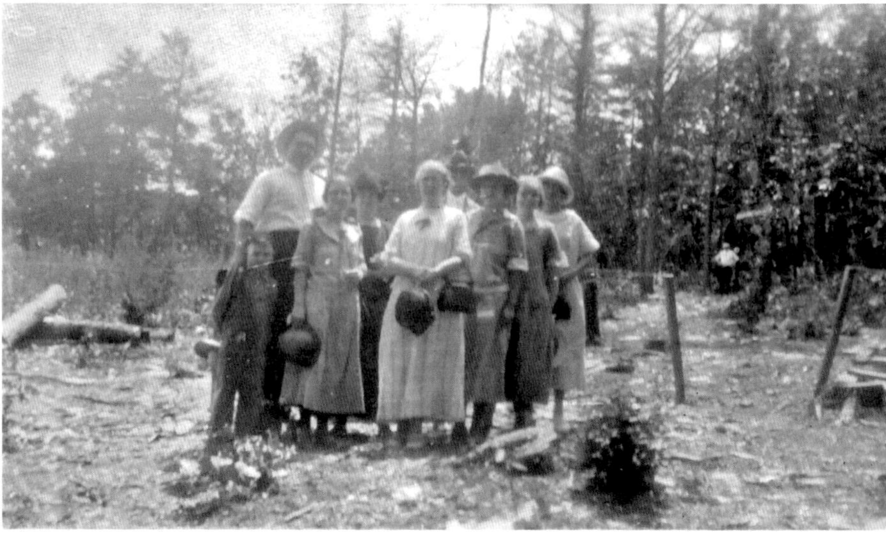

The Waughtown neighborhood where the chanting monks were heard.

chanting monks was unknown. The residents assumed they had moved on or were lost when the cavern was destroyed. Mr. Johns believed the evil that had attacked the area might have been related to previous tales told to us. As our journey into the unknown continues, more information of this supernatural evil will be revealed.

Chapter 19

The Haunted Painting

Caves, old miners, specters in windows, haunted graveyards and chanting monks—all of these are part of our next tale in Winston-Salem's haunted history. The relationship of art with our next story concerns events and places beyond Winston-Salem and beyond the time period of Salem's existence. The haunted painting arrived to the hamlet of Salem in its early days, and some swear it has never left.

The contents of the painting had its origin in sixteenth-century Britain, circa 1560. In 1542, King Henry VIII instigated the first Witchcraft Act. The majority of the people at that time could not read or write, and interpretation of the law and the Bible was only done by monks and priests. Between 1542 and 1735, five Witchcraft Acts were passed, and one by Elizabeth I had a death penalty attached to it as well. Along the way, the Witchcraft Acts were watered down. In a few domains, punishment and imprisonment for witchcraft, fortunetellers or magic for pay is still enforced. Returning to the sixteenth century, the traditional view of the book of Leviticus, compiled by Moses, was that it was the benchmark to determine the rules and regulations for witchcraft and the like. Priests and monks often quoted the Leviticus passages along with the enforcement carried out by the king or queen. Some of the more memorable quotes of Leviticus of the Old Testament had a strong impact in the creation of the haunted painting of our tale. Leviticus 19:20: "You shall not eat anything with the blood nor shall you practice divination or soothsaying." The practice of using animal parts in divination was common in the sixteenth century. Voodoo rituals still practice these divination ways. Leviticus 19:31 states: "Give no regard to mediums and familiar spirits; do not seek after them, to be defiled by them: I am the Lord your God." The haunted painting was engrained with familiar spirits, as depicted in scriptures, to a point that it took on a life of its own. Leviticus 20:6–8 speaks against spiritualism: "And the person who turns to mediums and familiar spirits, to prostitute himself with them, I will set my face against that person and cast him off from his people. Consecrate yourselves, therefore, and be holy, for I am the Lord your God. And you shall keep my statutes, and perform them; I am the Lord who sanctified you." The biblical death penalty is found in Leviticus 20:27: "A man or a woman who is a medium, or who has familiar spirits, shall surely be put to death; they shall stone them with stones. Then blood shall be upon them."

It is believed the haunted painting was created by a monk in the sixteen century. This was no ordinary monk but rather one possessed by an evil that nearly destroyed parts of Europe and eventually made its way to the United States and to Winston-Salem. If our readers have not already guessed, the haunted painting was alive.

Upon arriving in Salem, it was believed to been on one of the first wagon trains to pass through the brand-new Paper Mill Settlement of Old West Salem in 1790. How or why it ended up here is anyone's guess; however, the old-timers believed the painting may have been a gift—a dark gift—to a practicing witch who had escaped from England before she was executed for her crime, as stipulated in Leviticus. Mr. Johns believed the painting was given to the witch not as a gift but to keep it from being destroyed as well.

Reportedly, the witch continued on her journey with the wagon train and was never heard from again. The painting appeared to have stayed on its own choosing. Could this have been the original evil that plagued the area of Old West Salem and beyond? As a child, I had an additional question concerning the painting: "What was contained in the painting, and how was it alive?" The old-timer Mr. Johns answered:

> *My grandfather had an opportunity to get a peek of the painting of the Zinzendorf Resort Hotel that was built on the old Fries Plantation. My grandfather said it was a horrid thing. The painting appeared to come off the canvas. The description was as if it was three-dimensional, and the painting changed in the content of the figures. A person could view the painting from an angle and then move to another angle and the grotesque figures could change from an old hag to a cyclops or ogre entity. Much of the artwork was painted in several shades of red. My grandfather spoke*

to another patron, and the man nodded in agreement to his assessment: the painting appeared to have been painted in blood. My grandfather swore on a stack of Bibles that when he touched the cursed thing, it felt warm and pulsated as it was alive.

Mr. Johns's grandfather decided to come back the next day for another look to see if the painting might have changed again. Unfortunately, he never got a chance; the resort hotel burned to the ground that day. He watched the fire from the park, Grace Court Park in today's landscape, across the street from the hotel. Supposedly, very little was saved or salvaged from the fire. The rambling wooden Victorian structure burned instantly. The fire

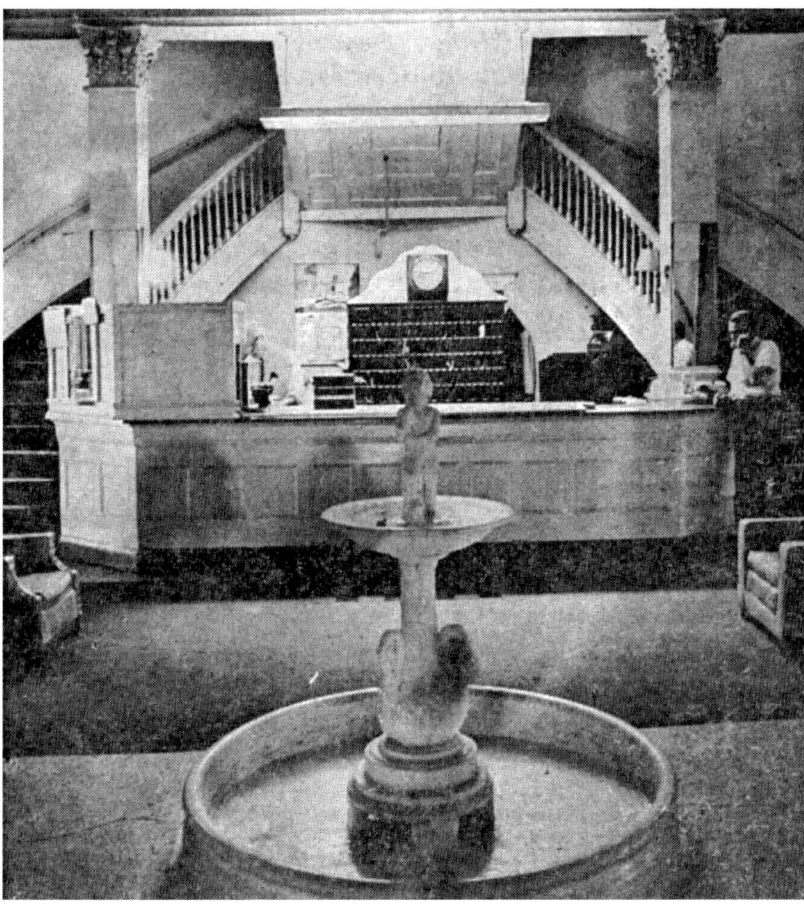

The desk of the second Zinzendorf Hotel on North Mail Street circa 1900 and the second home of the haunted painting.

department was Johnny-on-the-spot; however, their hoses were too short to reach the hydrants. The city passed an ordinance after the fire. No large structures or buildings ever from that time forward could be built in that construction. The days of the rambling Victorian wooden mansions were over. As for the haunted painting, it survived, though no one knew how. The fire was determined an accident with no probable cause. Many suspected arson; some suspected the haunted painting.

The painting reappeared at the new and modern second Zinzendorf Hotel, downtown on Main Street. Two paintings were displayed, one of the Kaiser of Germany and the other the painting of our tale. Several years later, the United States entered World War I with Germany, and the Kaiser painting was covered over with wallpaper. The haunted painting vanished. It surprisingly resurfaced at a private home at the corner of Spring Street and West Fourth Street in the Old West End. Mr. Johns's brother knew the owner of the homeplace and had the pleasure of viewing the painting there. The owner had bought the painting at a private auction. He claimed that he did not know why he bought the artwork—only that he was mysteriously drawn to it. He informed Mr. Johns's brother that he and his family were in the process of selling the painting since strange things had been happening around the house.

Mr. Johns's brother enquired about the strange events and was given this story:

> *I had displayed the painting in my study off of the dining room. The painting was framed in a three-foot by two-foot wooden frame, and I hung the artwork over the fireplace. I became mesmerized by the painting. It seemed to take on a life of its own, constantly changing the placement of its characters throughout the picture. It displayed an array of colors that seemed to hypnotize me as well. Do not think me insane, but by the second week the painting had been displayed, the characters became grotesque. They began to get on my nerves, but I was still drawn to it. Then one dark evening as I worked in my study, I began to hear voices. I thought that strange since I was the only one home. The voices were coming from the painting. I could not make out the words, so I placed my ear directly on the painting. Then someone or something poked my ear, cutting the lower part of my ear. I wiped the ear, and the small amount of blood on the painting seemed to change the painting somehow. By this time the characters in the painting had changed to witches, ghouls, and monsters, vial creatures that literally turned my stomach.*

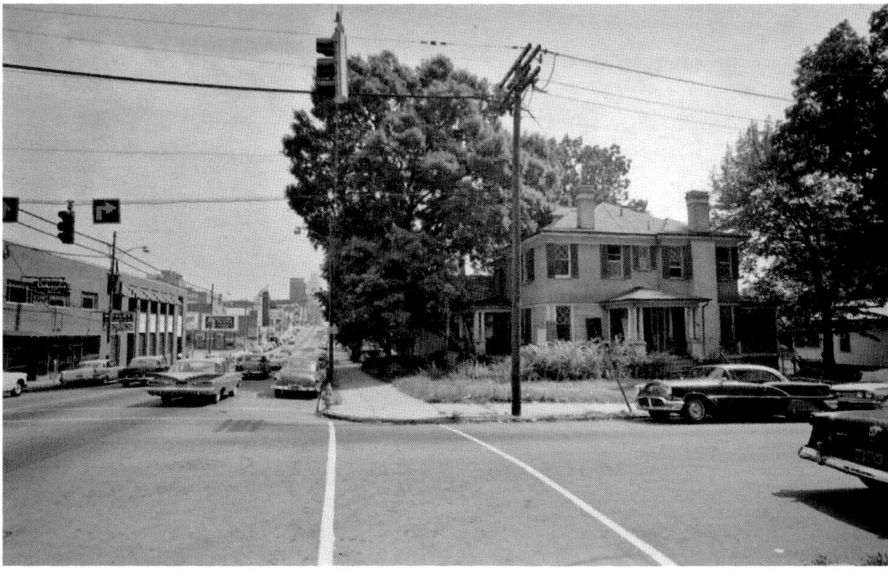

The old mansion at West Fourth Street and North Spring Street, the third location of the haunted painting.

Mr. John's brother said after gaining his composure, the man began to hear very distinct, guttural voices saying, "We are coming for you and your family, tonight." The owner decided at that very minute to destroy the painting. He gripped the poker from the fireplace and began to hammer viciously against the painting, slashing and stabbing it with every stroke of the poker. He was in a mortal rage—when suddenly he realized the painting had not even a scratch on the cursed thing. He then took the poker and carefully tried to make a scratch on one small section of the artwork. To his horror, as he watched, the painting magically repaired itself. He then tried to rip the ugly thing from the wall, but it would not budge. He had heard stories of this painting from others who had encountered it, but now he knew the truth was even worse. He left the room and rounded up his family and exited the premises. He and his family stayed with a family friend the next night.

With several of his friends, he reentered the house on the second day after the terrible incident. The house was locked up, as he had left it previously. As the clan entered the mansion, a burning smell permeated the house. To the group's amazement, the painting and its frame had disappeared from the wall. The smell was identified as burning flesh by one of the man's friends who had served in the First World War and remembered the smell from the battlefield.

The haunted painting was not seen again, according to Mr. Johns. A question had plagued Mr. Johns for several years thereafter. If the haunted painting had been destroyed, and the inhabitants of the painting were real and the smell of burning flesh was throughout the homestead, could the beings in the painting have escaped, and the evil that was trapped along with them also become free? Only in future tales of the unknown will the answer be found.

Chapter 20

The Game That Would Not End

The all-American game of baseball has been a part of Winston-Salem since its early beginnings. The sandlot games of our youth were played in ball fields across the city, whether they were back street lots or city landscaped ball fields. Our tale concerns a group of ballplayers who began a game that extended beyond the grave.

The history of baseball in Winston-Salem began in the nineteenth century. One of the earliest teams was the Winston Blues. The 1888 team was quite colorful in name: "Big Liston," pitcher; "Shorty Jones," end-fielder; "Kid Farrell," second baseman; "Gigg McMann," shortstop; and "Ready Sand," captain, just to name a few. With the creation of the National Association of Baseball Teams in 1900, the modern era of baseball began. In 1905, Winston-Salem joined the Virginia–North Carolina Pro League. This league lasted one year. It was replaced by the old Carolina League in 1906. The league lasted through the 1916 season and ended because of America's entry into World War I.

The professional team moved around the city over the years. The team played its first years at the old Liberty Street ballpark, located where Sixteenth Street lies between Liberty Street at the Norfolk and Western Railroad. It moved to the old Piedmont Park fairgrounds in 1910 and continued the 1911 season at Prince Albert Park, located where American Bakeries Plant at Liberty Street and Twelfth Street. The Prince Albert Park continued the league play until the old Southside Park opened in 1921 near Gray High School, currently the site of the North Carolina School of the Arts off South

Main Street. Southside Park was destroyed by fire in the 1920s and was rebuilt shortly thereafter. The old, rebuilt Southside field met its fate in 1955 with a double punch of fire and a windstorm. This led to the building of the historic Ernie Shore Field on Thirtieth Street.

Professional baseball has come full circle throughout Winston-Salem and exits today at the BB&T ball field at Peters Creek Parkway in the heart of old West Salem. The professional baseball teams in Winston-Salem have always had a following with the general populace of the city, especially with the children.

However, our tale begins with another group of ballplayers between 1900 and the 1920s. One of the most colorful periods of local baseball began with the semipro teams in 1900. Our first was the Winston Blues, mentioned earlier in the story. The team had its home plate on Patterson Avenue, just across from the old armory building on Liberty Street. Judge Gideon Hastings pitched for the Blues, and Judge Tom Walser played as well.

With the dawn of the new century, the neighborhoods of Winston and Salem became a part of this colorful semipro league. In 1906, those neighborhood teams were added, and boy, could they play, according to the

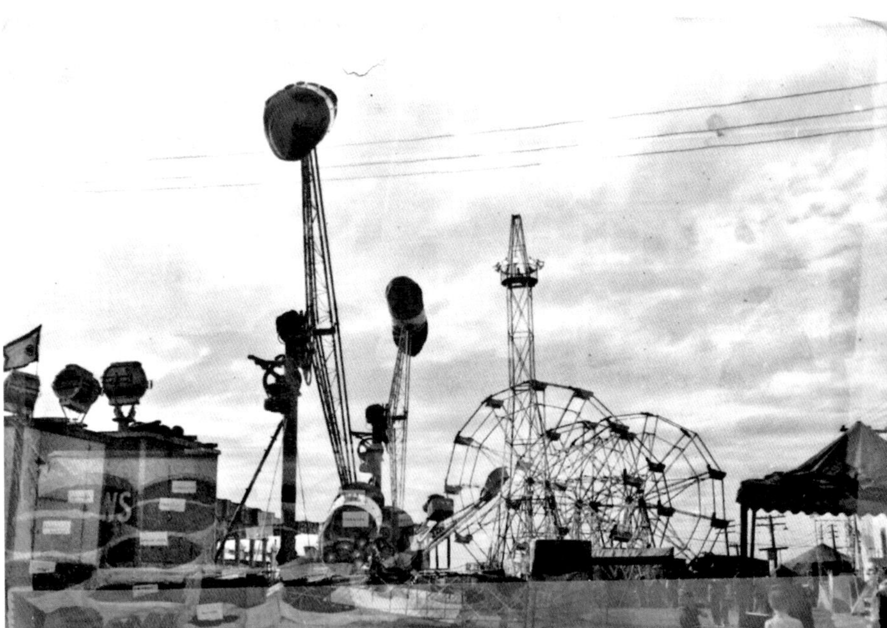

In 1908, North Liberty Street became the location of the Winston-Salem fairgrounds and ball field. This ball field was the scene of the tale of the last ballplayers, as well as the appearance of the great Babe Ruth.

old-timers of the Green Front Cash Store. The Waughtown Wild Cats were considered the best. The old-timers stated that their games were fantastic to watch, and as they were the local boys of the area, it made it even better. Over a period of years, the Wild Cats accumulated a record unmatched even in the professional national league. They had sixty wins and only three losses. Those three losses came at the hands of pitchers who played in the pro league. Mr. John noted, "I believe the semipro Waughtown Wild Cats could have beat any professional national league team on a given day if they were on their game, for sure."

The Salem Stars arrived in 1906—and "they were not pushovers either," another old-timer chimed in. Even our own West Salem was not left behind. The West Salem Stars was a scrappy group and could hold their own with any team, the old-timers added. The games were played at several locations. The Waughtown Wild Cats arrived to their games decked out in blue uniforms with blue-and-white stockings. Their home diamond was in Southside, where Trinity Moravian Church is currently located. A second backup sandlot was located on Stadium Drive. The Salem Red Socks had several sandlots behind homes on Main Street and Liberty Street. The West Salem Red Socks played in back lots supplied by the Brietz and Leinbach families. In 1913, the playground and ball field of Granville Graded School was used extensively for many semipro baseball games on Saturday afternoons.

These were wonderful times of youth, sports and overall well-being for the citizens of these older neighborhoods. Those who played were admired by their parents, relatives and youngsters, who attempted to mimic them on the field. The players from the Waughtown Wild Cats, the Salem Stars, the Winston Blues and the West Salem Red Socks became the major players of the game that would not end. The team members included Will Vogler, Sid Teague, Fate McGee, Tip Crowder, Luther Charles, Carl Nissen, Frank Nissen, Gene Vogler, John Henry Hemrick, Dewey Kiser, Dewey Faircloth, Gene Adams, Rube Hartness, John Sappenfield, Jim Boles and the Hutchins boys of Southside. The old-timers said there were more players, but these were some they knew personally.

The league stopped with the advent of World War I. In 1917, many of the names above were called for service in the military, and many more names were called by their maker. The darkness of the war and its losses, multiplied by the great flu epidemic of 1918, took its toll on the baseball league, which closed until 1920. The war's losses and the masses of death attributed to the epidemic drew a dark, frightening cloud over the country.

The same solemn and depressed atmosphere of the country radiated throughout Winston-Salem, even into the children. Some children believed the baseball days of their heroes were over, along with any chance for their future. An event occurred that brought a silver lining to that dark cloud, and the aftereffects of the event changed the future for the children and baseball alike. Mr. Johns quoted the sportswriter of the day at this event that brought the silver lining:

> *Probably one of the greatest baseball days in Winston-Salem history occurred on April 8, 1920, when Ernie Shore, the Yadkin County right-hander, came back home to pitch the New York Yankees to a 3-0 exhibition game victory over Brooklyn. The game was played at the old fairgrounds on North Liberty Street. More than ten thousand fans attended. Babe Ruth, who most called the best hitter of a baseball in the history of the game to present time, hit his longest ball on record, 650 feet. No other human on record to this day has ever hit one farther. Many of the local semipro boys of Waughtown, Salem and West Salem teams were on hand. Several of the group reported to their friends a strange occurrence happened at the ballpark that day. Near the dugout, over to the right from where the ball boys and players practiced, a small gang of boys sat watching the game. The group in the stands swore they could identify the boys near the dugout as former ballplayers in the league.*

This was very scary for the ballplayers in the stands. The boys they had identified were lost during the war and the flu epidemic. They were dead. The former ballplayers in the stand were dumbfounded and proceeded to the dugout to see if their eyes were deceiving them. These deceased ballplayers could not be found. By the time the former ballplayers arrived at the dugout, the group of lost ballplayers had simply disappeared. They inquired to the ball boys and the other players who were practicing near the dugout if they had seen this gang of boys watching the game. They were shocked and dismayed by the response: "No one is allowed down in the dugout, only the players. There were no boys here."

The group believed the late boyhood friends were ghosts who visited the historic game to see the best hitter who ever played the game here in Winston-Salem. The boys' connection to baseball was so important in life that it followed them in death. The boys were looking forward to the beginning of baseball season several weeks after the completion of the professional game with Babe Ruth. They had practiced with the Waughtown Wild Cats during spring training. It was getting late, and they were heading back home after practice. Most of these players lived in old West Salem. As they passed Granville School, they noticed lights behind the school at the park and ball field. In 1920, there was no outside lighting at the school.

What they witnessed next helped to reclaim the game and put the spark back into the players. The lost boys of baseball were playing the last ball game they had hoped to play before they died unexpectedly. The smile on their faces was heart-warming. The group of ballplayers joined with their former lost comrades in order to continue the game that would not end.

Chapter 21

The Hermit of Shallowford Street

First Street, the dividing line between Winston and Salem, has brought some strange stories so far in our journey into the unknown. This one, I believe, is unique to our tales in that it profiles the hope and beauty of life. My personal journey and that of my boyhood friends led to an understanding that life is so precious and should never be taken for granted. As the Bible says and as is often quoted, always be aware of those around you, as you may be entertaining angels in disguise.

The intersections of Broad Street today (formerly Old Shallowford Road, circa 1765), Brookstown Avenue today, (New Shallowford Road, circa 1840s) and First Street today (North Street Circa 1830s) were the crossroads of travelers traversing between Winston and Salem from 1849—Winston's creation—to 1913, when Winston and Salem officially merged to become one town. Foot traffic, wagons, buggies and every other type of transportation flowed through here. Even a haunted Nissen wagon passed through these crossroads in an earlier tale. In 1964, however, an individual arrived in my neighborhood who was different from any other individual, I believe, who ever passed through these crossroads in more than 250 years.

Our tale starts with an introduction to my boyhood friends in the crossroad neighborhood. John and David Ferriaolo resided at 703 Shallowford Street with their mother and father, Virginia and Salvador. Their dad was Italian and had arrived to America with his family from Italy in the early 1900s. Their mother was a natural-born citizen. The couple met in Connecticut when both worked in an ammunition factory during the Second World

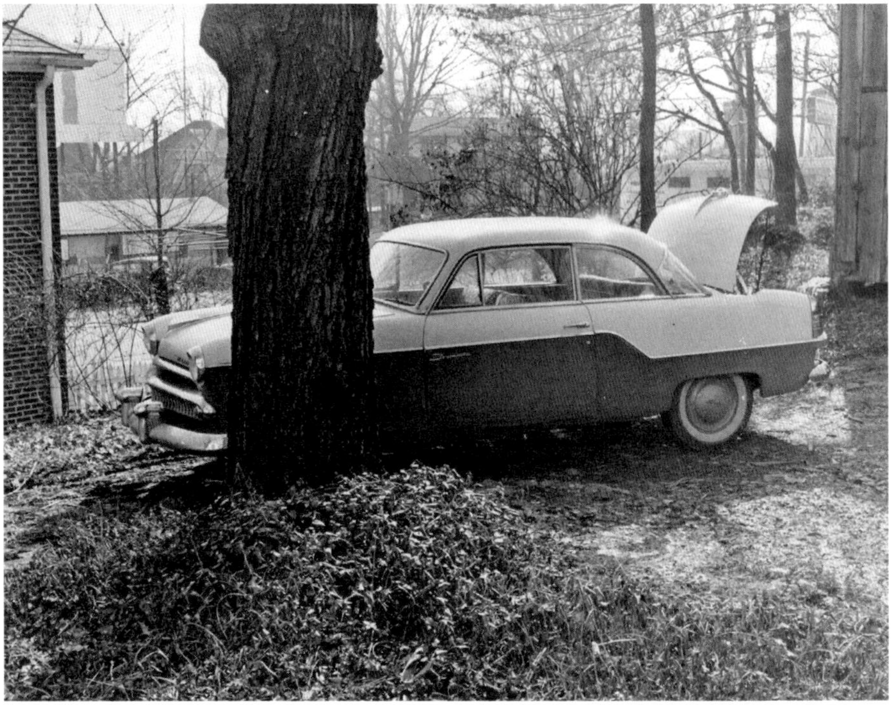

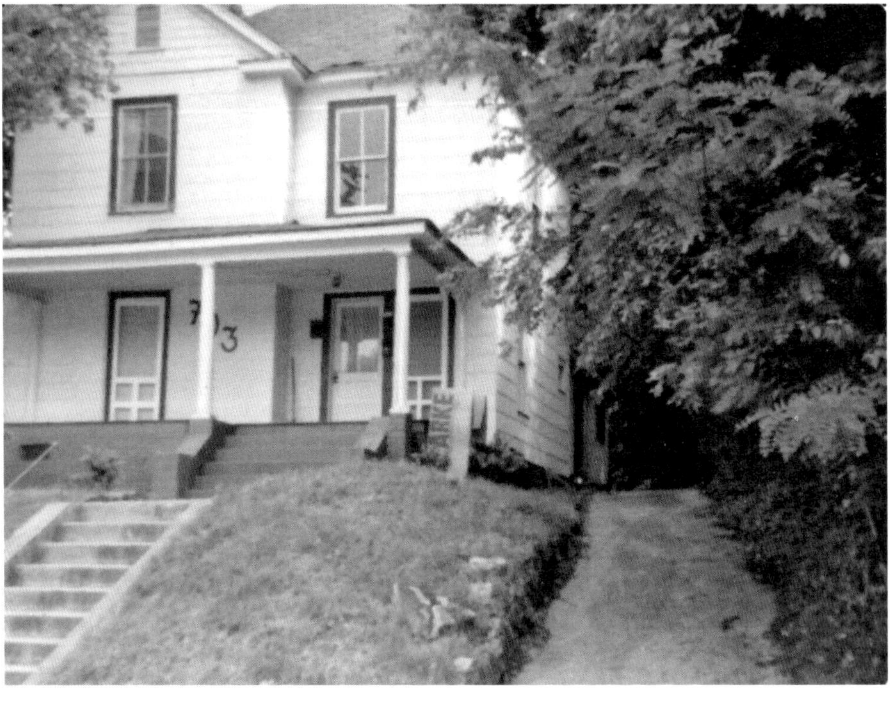
703

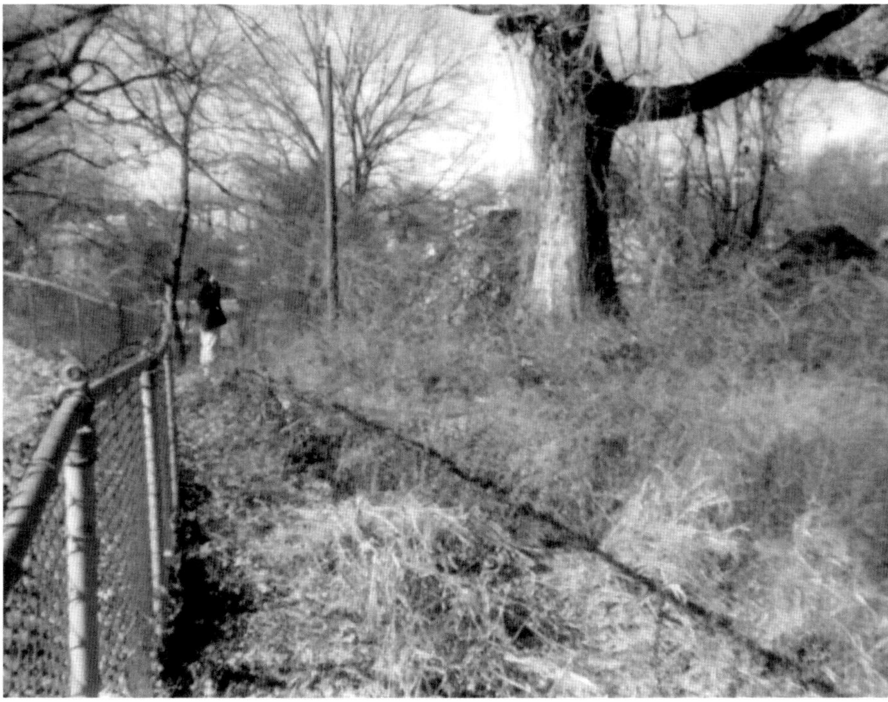

The road to Salem, Old Shallowford Road is shown with one of the remaining trees being photographed for prosperity.

Opposite, top: The backyard of Mr. Frank Jones, a photographer for more than forty years for the *Winston-Salem Journal* and a regular at the Green Front Cash Store, is shown, with Old Shallowford Street behind.

Opposite, bottom: This circa 1970s photo depicts 703 Shallowford Street, home of David and John Ferriaolo, next to the Hermit of Shallowford Street's hideout. In today's landscape, a flight of stairs to 703 Shallowford is all that remains of this story.

War. The family arrived to the crossroads in 1962. My family arrived to the crossroads in 1957, living at 114 North Broad Street, across from the Green Front Cash Store, the centerpoint of our woven tales. My family moved here from Old Salem on Main Street after the interstate road system destroyed the total block for the Business Interstate Road system of today. Nearly one hundred homes and business were lost and destroyed in Salem during the building of the roadway in the 1950s—an ironic twist of fate connecting the road system of Interstate 40 and Old West Salem.

The interstate system, once completed, connected the East Coast with the West Coast. In Old West Salem, the Paper Mill Settlement connected settlers to their future homes across the expanse of the country, and Henderson Lewellen, the "Johnny Appleseed" of Old West Salem, created horticulture centers and founded towns that he called Salem across America as well. His last stop was Salem, Oregon, the capital, and currently the number-one horticulture center of the United States.

Our home at 114 North Broad Street had a history of its own. The house was the residence and business of Mr. Thomas Butner. The Butner family were original Moravians of Salem. Mr. Butner's family was associated with the first suburb of Salem in an earlier tale. His residence and business at 114 North Broad Street was home to the Lone Star Poultry Farm circa 1840s. The business lasted until 1910. A salvaged junkyard and leftovers from the farm found in the block bordered by Brookstown Avenue, First Street and Broad Street were believed by the old-timers to be hidden under the pavement of later built businesses. Currently, the block has been sold to the developers of the BB&T ball field complex for future development of the crossroads. The old-timers also believe if the pavement is ever taken up, hidden treasures or an abandoned graveyard could be found.

My family homestead at 114 North Broad Street, often called the Barn, was heated by several potbellied stoves, which were the cooking and heating source of the 1840 house. We moved one block over to 119 South Broad Street in 1960. This homestead was one of the mansions built on South Broad Street in 1918. The home was originally built for a doctor who ran the tuberculosis sanatorium of Winston-Salem. Our home was located around the corner from 703 Shallowford Street, the Ferriaolo home. Old Shallowford Street was cut in the 1850s as a connector street to the Old Plank Road, Brookstown Avenue today. Before the arrival of our main character of our story, my friends and I were typical boys of the 1960s who were fortunate enough to live centrally at the some of the most historic roads of North Carolina. Our historic downtown of the 1960s had been left behind in the creation of the shopping centers of the 1950s. This was a plus for my friends and I in the crossroads neighborhood. Our families could shop, go to movies and explore the old roads and buildings of Historic Winston without all the crowds of the shopping centers. To the south was Old Salem, and exploration of the emerging restored town and the old parts that preceded the restoration could be found as well.

My friends and our families often socialized on the "patio," as we called it. The paved flattop, the patio, was built over several garages at 119 South Broad Street, the old doctor's former home. The garage had kept several of the doctor's vehicles. A T-model Ford and even a buggy from the early

1900s were stored here. The garage stretched for nearly half a block down Shallowford Street. The mansion of the doctor was a three-story, stucco and pebble-dash structure, a style that was popular in the early 1900s. Since Broad Street sat on the topmost section of the Old Shallowford ridge, the steep drop from the ridge down to the bottom of Old Shallowford Street was the equivalent to a five- or six-story building in the change of elevation.

The drop from the patio to the sidewalk below on Shallowford Street was the equivalent to one-story—ten feet. Our main character of the tale had its encounter with us here, an encounter that both thrilled and terrified us boys one dark night. The elements of the Halloween season of 1964 were like many others previous—trick or treat, things that go bump in the night, the autumn leaves covering the ground and the wonderful bare spooky trees. Trees, hundreds of years old, honeycombed throughout the crossroads of the neighborhood. We often sat on the porch or the patio and imagined the trees at Halloween as grotesque and ghoulish creatures because of their twisted shapes. We always hoped for something different and more shocking and mysterious with every Halloween. In 1964, got our wish.

That October, the air was more brisk and the winds felt more like winter. The fall leaves were blown around immensely on that sinister night two days before Halloween. Our gang was sitting on the patio, planning our agenda for Halloween night, which just so happened to fall on Friday this year.

We did not know it then, but this evening was our first encounter with the hermit. The patio was across the street from a local eatery. Parkers Drive-In was a 1950s-style restaurant that was popular during this time period with its drive-up parking, complete with the proverbial carhop. That night, the neon lights of the establishment cast a strange light across the old garages below the patio. As we planned the Halloween events, an odd shadow caught our eyes as it moved across the sidewalk below. Often neighbors strolled along this stretch of pavement, but this time was different. Once we saw the figure, its size overwhelmed us. The figure had a gate that our fastest runner could not match. The height of the head of the entity was less than three inches below the patio. Remember that the height from where we were standing to the sidewalk below, where the thing was walking, was ten feet. As the creature continued on its journey, never acknowledging us, we were mesmerized, frozen as the mannequins in the windows of the downtown stores. By the time we gained our composure, the entity was gone. We ran down the steps from the patio to Shallowford Street and up the hill to Broad Street to try to follow the path of the creature, but it had disappeared, and no trace could be found.

For the rest of the evening, we discussed this invader to the crossroads. Ideas and boyhood fantasies from science fiction movies and the like gave us possible explanations for what we had just witnessed. This was no movie; the creature was flesh and bone—no specter, no phantom, no space man.

For the next two days, we polled our neighborhood friends and families to see if they knew of this thing we saw. None had, and most said we were merely creating a Halloween stunt.

Halloween came and went. Don't get me wrong, it was great—but the only thing John and David and the rest of us had on our minds was to get to the bottom of this mystery.

The path to finding the creature began a week later. On Old Shallowford Street, below patio garages, existed four homes. The first was a 1930, two-story structure with a front porch. The second was an empty, rundown Victorian-style homeplace. We entered the creepy place, the old haunted house, which had a wraparound porch. The old-timers said this was a pre–Civil War mansion, one of the original home sites that was built next to the Old Plank Road. Next to this house was the Ferriaolo home, a late nineteenth-century structure that had been moved from across the street in the 1940s for the creation of the block for the Parkers Drive-In establishment in the late 1940s.

John and David had noticed strange occurences next door at the haunted house. Spooky lights, voices and objects around the outside of the house were seen and heard. The parents of John and David thought hobos or vagrants may have taken up roost in the old house. We were told not to mess around the old structure; it was not safe. We decided this could be the location of the creature's hideout.

The next day was Saturday, and our plan was to find the creature and check out the haunted house. We met early at 703 Shallowford Street and cautiously crept to the edge of the haunted property, where we froze with fear. Hanging on an old decaying tree branch was a noose—a hanging noose. We had only seen this scene in cowboy movies. Old writings, which we could not read or understand, were carved in the tree. One carved item we did know was a skull and cross bones. We determined that someone or something did not want us here. Curiosity may have killed the cat, but we boys were only driven further on our mission. We walked around the entire house and to the backyard. A small road existed behind the 1930 home next to the haunted house. I discovered later that it was an old nineteenth-century roadbed that connected North Spring Street to South Spring Street on the other side of Interstate 40.

Once on the wraparound front porch, we found a door that was not locked and proceeded to enter the old house. Cobwebs, musty smells and old newspapers covered the walls and floors of the house. We realized after reading several of the newspapers lying around that no one had lived here in years. The newspapers were from the 1930s, thirty years in the past. Some old cots covered in dust were found as well. Over the next weeks, the Ferriaolo family continued to hear moaning sounds and undistinguishable conversations and saw spooky lights from the old mansion. The police were called by the residents on the other side of the old place because they saw a rather tall man with a long scraggly beard going into the old structure. No one was found, but the description matched closely what we had witnessed that first night. We never knew what happened to the creature, and as November ended, we simply moved on. Thanksgiving was coming and Christmas was not far behind.

However, one cold snowy day, our crossroads neighborhood experienced a terrible fire. The old haunted house was reduced to cinders, and only two massive chimneys like giant obelisks remained. Thank goodness the houses on either side of the burned structure were not harmed. One last time before the debris of the house was hauled to the dump, we entered the property of the century-old structure to see if any sign of man or beast could be found. One may think this was last chance of finding the Hermit of Shallowford; however, what happened at Christmas of 1964 changed the boys of Shallowford Street forever.

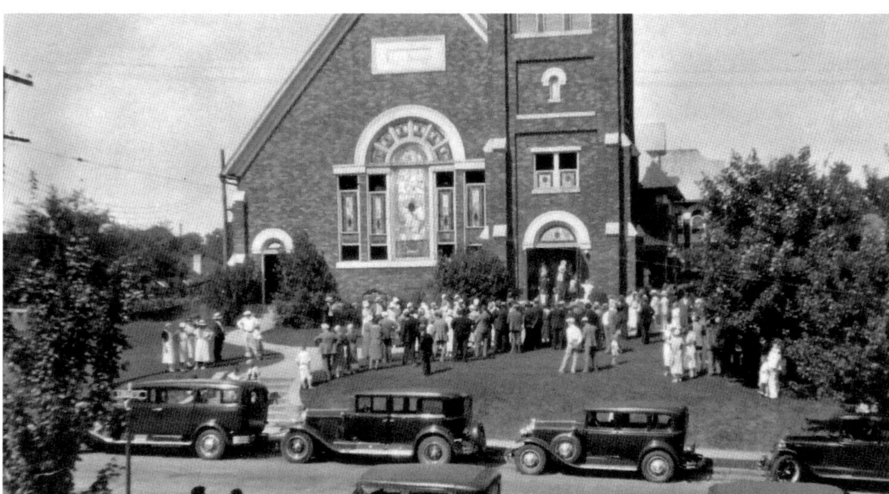

Salem Baptist Church, circa 1920s.

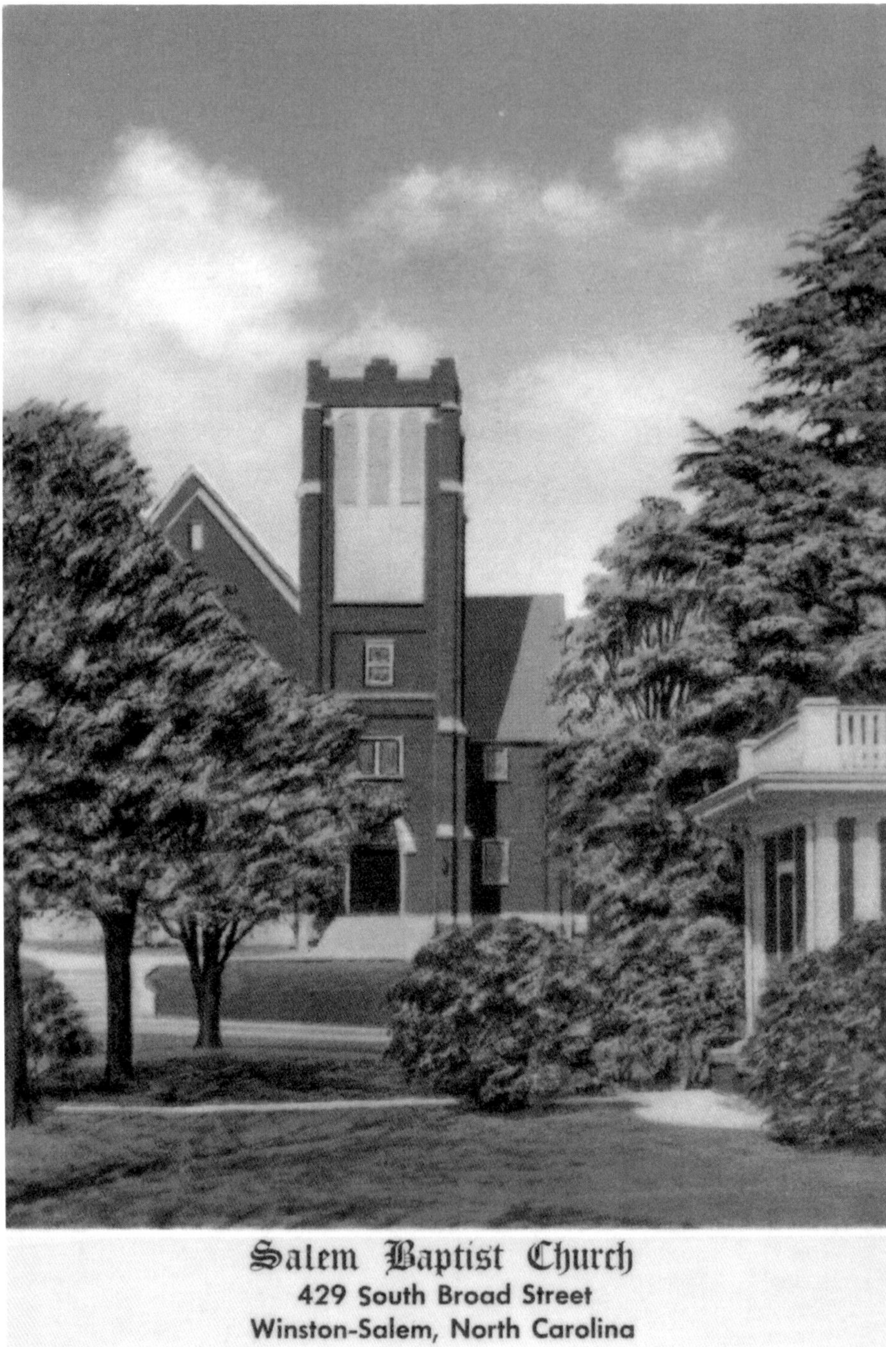

Salem Baptist Church, circa 1918.

Christmas Eve service was to be held at my grandmother's church in Old West Salem, Salem Baptist Church. Everyone was invited—Baptist, Methodist, Lutheran, Moravian, nondenominational or no denomination. Everyone was welcome to the Christmas service. Up Shallowford Street, along Broad Street south, our parents, grandparents and friends of the crossroads all traveled the four blocks to the church. Dr. Charles Stevens was the pastor. The old sanctuary, built in 1918, was decorated beautifully. The smell of holiday treats drifted throughout the church, enticing us children. We had already been given our instructions by the elders to be seen and not heard, except, of course, during songs. The pastor had just began with a prayer when silence overcame the whole sanctuary.

The pastor paused, as did all others. Upon turning of my head, I realized why. Entering the church and proceeding down the long central aisle was the largest and tallest person I have ever seen to this day. He ducked his head as in reverence to the church, not in prayer, but to keep from striking his head on the balcony overhanging the sanctuary. The Guinness Book of World Records states that Robert Waldlow is the tallest man on record to this day, at eight feet and eleven inches. He would have made over nine feet if he had not died of a foot infection. The hermit had returned, and from his stature, he was well over nine feet tall. His beard was as white as snow, not as dark as it appeared in our first encounter. He spoke not a word, but with a smile on his face, he sat down quietly in a pew two rows back from mine. The adults appeared to become uneasy, including the pastor and the elders. The young people and especially the children blurted out several times to their parents, "Look, there is Santa Claus!"

The service continued after the adults silenced the little ones. The hermit stood and sang with the most beautiful baritone voice the congregation had ever heard. The hermit did not have a music book; rather, he seemed to know every song by heart. Just before the service ended, the hermit instantly arose and turned down the aisle from where he had come. The congregation was frozen with awe as the hermit exited the church. As the door closed behind the hermit, the children ran from their pews, calling, "Santa Claus, please come back!"

Before the adults and elders could realize it, the children had left the building. I was already heading behind the children as well. What I saw and what my friends saw as we stood beside the church were the children gathered around the tall figure of a man as he sat on the wall outside the church. He smiled and spoke these words to all: "I am the old elf, Santa Claus, but to ye children tonight my father and yours is the Lord, bless you all." The hermit arose, and with the stride we had witnessed that first night when he had disappeared on Broad Street, he very quickly disappeared, headed back to the old house on Shallowford Street. The hermit of Shallowford was truthfully not a creature but a saint.

Chapter 22

The Poor Little Lost Boy

Our next tale is sad and terrifying. The loss of a child includes both of these emotions and many more. For a parent to be separated from their children in a physical way by abduction is only compounded when that abduction extends from the physical world into the supernatural one. This story was originally touched on by the old-timers at the Green Front Cash Store. They knew of the terrible loss but not the in-depth facts. In the early 1970s, I had the privilege to meet and get to know one of the most interesting characters I have ever known. He supplied the facts of our story.

Mr. George Starling was an amazing man. He had created his own business and traveled all over the state peddling his wares—oh, and by the way, he had been blind from birth. He taught himself the Braille language and along the way developed a love of music. He taught piano and became the first blind piano salesman in the state. He was always very independent and did not let his loss of sight hinder him. Mr. Starling often reflected to his customers, myself being one. His family had always told him the loss of sight was a blessing. If he had not been blind, he believed as well, his life would not have turned out in such a positive way. With all his faculties, he may not have developed the appreciation for life that allowed him to be strong enough to survive his youth.

As a young apprentice in the piano business, he worked with Mr. Bowen. The Bowen piano company was one of the best-known and most respected piano dealerships in Winston-Salem. This was a third-generation family company begun in the early 1900s by Mr. Bowen's grandfather. Mr. Bowen

PAGE 26 —— WEDNESDAY EVENING, MAY 4, 1960

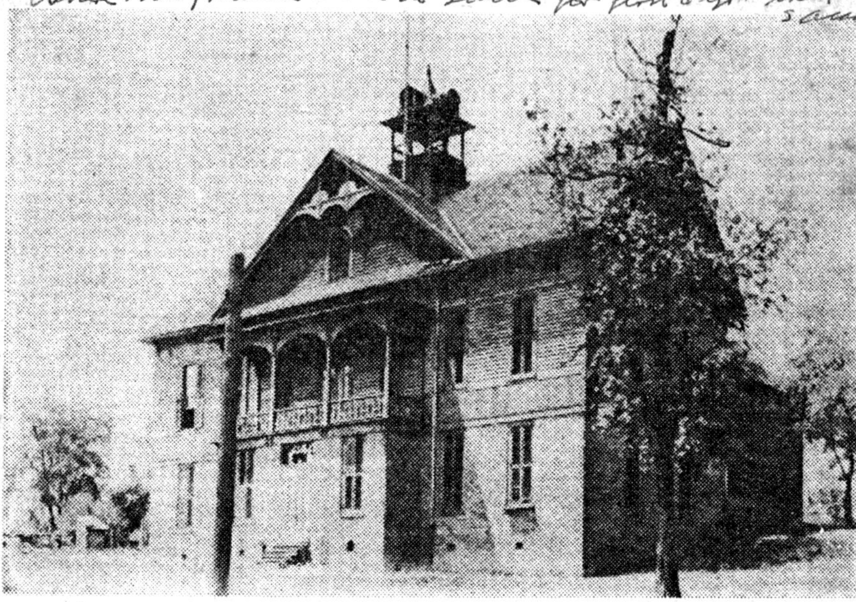

Do You Remember . . .

By BILL EAST
Sentinel City Editor

The West Salem School (above) already was an old institution when a young principal arrived in 1911 to take over. He was W. B. Clinard.

Clinard, now retired after 33 years as a principal and living at 2252 Elizabeth Avenue, recalled yesterday that the school occupied a 200 by 200-foot lot facing Mulberry Street with Laurel Street at the rear. Academy Street ran alongside the building.

The school, which had five classrooms and a large assembly room, was part of the Forsyth County system until Winston and Salem were merged in 1913.

At that time, the Winston-Salem school system was organized. It immediately started hunting for a site for a new school in the West Salem area.

The school system obtained a 300 by 300-foot lot on Granville Driv[illegible] from the Moravians. Work was starte[illegible] on a new school building.

The picture of the [illegible]st Salem School shown above was believed to have been taken about 1915—the year that it was abandoned in favor of Granville.

Clinard said the new school was named after the street which ran in front of it, "although Granville Nading, who lived nearby, said he thought it was named for him."

On moving day, Clinard recalled that he had the larger boys in the old school carry the desks four blocks westward to the new Granville School "because we already had new desks and didn't want to get them scratched on a moving wagon."

Later, another 300 by 300-foot lot was obtained from the Moravians to form the present Granville School playgrounds. The city purchased the land later to establish tennis courts a short distance away.

After his arrival from High Point to take over his school job here, Clinard met the principal of the East Salem School on Belews Street—Maude Alspaugh. They were married in 1913. Afterward, she continued teaching for some time in the schools here.

Old West Salem Graded School, circa 1895.

and young Mr. Starling were the first to invent a one-person piano mover. When Mr. Starling was showing his talents in loading and unloading a one-thousand-pound piano alone, he usually joked with his customers, saying, "If the boss man let me, this old blind man would drive as well."

Our story of the poor little lost boy was related to me by Mr. Starling at his piano shop located on South Broad Street at the corner of Academy Street. He remembered the park and playground of the West Salem School after the school had been torn down. The city and its churches used the park and playground for social events. He said he already felt a close connection to the tale since his family knew many of the families at the mill, and their children attended the West Salem Graded School (circa 1895) and Granville Graded School (circa 1913), which replaced it.

This tale began at the old park at an event sponsored by a neighborhood church. The principal character in our story was a boy named Billy. He was believed to have been in the first class of the new Granville Graded School, circa 1913. His parents were textile workers employed at the Arista Cotton Mill, circa 1880s. The Baptist Mission Church on Marshall Street had been built circa 1900 with the help of the boss weaver of Arista Mills, Brother Sam Morton, and Broad Street Baptist Church on North Broad Street. The Baptist Mission Church was the family church of Billy.

The time period was the summer of 1916, and the event was a tent revival with a picnic and games at the playground for the children. Well-known evangelists were guest speakers, and Mr. Starling believed this speaker to be either Billy Sunday or Mordecai Ham. In the late afternoon, Billy Sunday would appear at church. He was a national Baptist minister, who often debated the evolution theory throughout the 1920s. Mordecai Ham was also a national Baptist minister, who—legend has it—saved and baptized the world-renowned Baptist minister Reverend Billy Graham.

The summer afternoon revival was multifunctional for the mill. The supervisor of the mill was attending and allowed the mill workers to slow its production so as many workers as possible could attend the service. The children were supervised by volunteer teachers of Granville Graded School so the adults could concentrate on the revival. The national known evangelist had not only been welcomed by the church sponsor but also by the city leaders. Several of the city leaders, including the mayor and city council members, were in attendance. This was a political/media opportunity that the city could not pass up. Separation of church and state was not existent at this revival.

As late afternoon arrived, the Mission Baptist revival came to an end. The adult family members ventured to the playground to be reunited with their

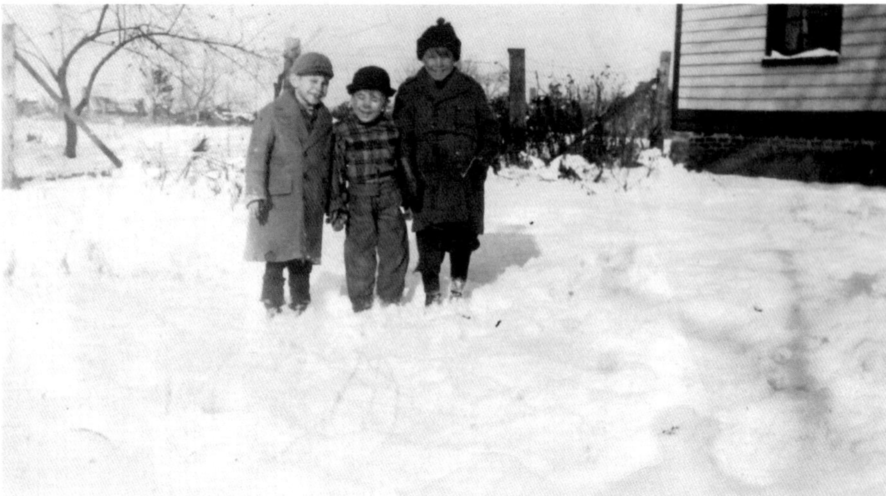

Brietz kids and friends who attended West Salem Graded School with the lost boy circa 1914.

children and join in the festivities of the church refreshments. Unfortunately, a tale of heartache and sacrifice replaced the festivities when the family of Billy realized he was gone. His parents searched high and low. They asked everyone—the grade school teachers, friends and their children—but no one had seen Billy in a long while. They finally found a young female classmate who said she saw Billy with an older gentleman but did not know him. After that, she did not know what happened to Billy. The picnic was eventually cancelled and the search continued for Billy. The police arrived and took statements from those who attended.

Mr. Starling believed kidnapping was involved, but oddly, weeks later, it was determined to stop the investigation because a scandal had developed. The city and a prominent national evangelist were connected to the revival, and the missing child made for bad political ties since there had been a kidnapping investigation.

With the official end of the investigation and the manhunt over, the parents were left with the heartache of a missing son. The parents spent all their waking days searching for their son. They lost their jobs at the textile mill, they lost their residence since it was connected to the mill and they left the city in total despair and frustration. They refused to believe the talk throughout the city that their son was dead, probably murdered. For a short time after their departure, a friend from the mill who had kept in touch with them by mail related to the others in town that the couple had split up

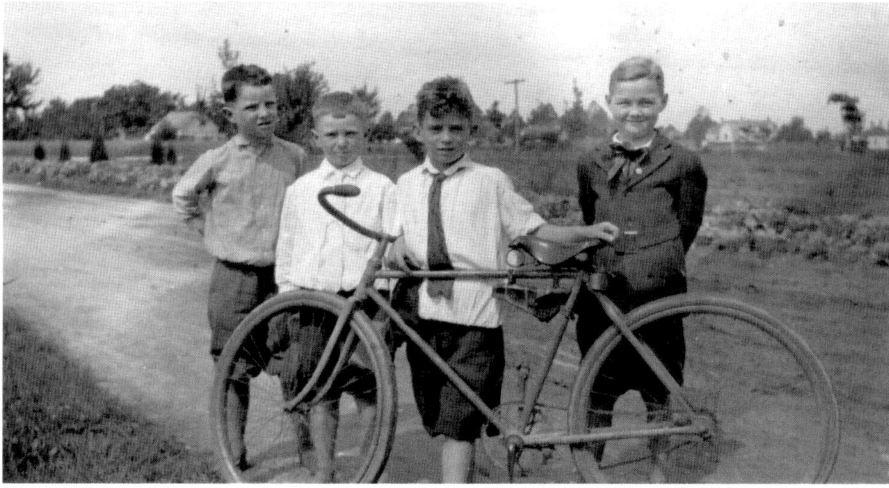

Broad Street circa 1914, before the modern road paving of the late 1910s and 1920s.

after depression and grief had riddled them. Later, the town heard that the couple's health had failed and both ended up at the county home in their new community.

Nearly a year passed, and the lost boy became a footnote of past news. Supernatural occurrences began to occur throughout the neighborhood of Old West Salem. The first was experienced by several close friends of the boys' parents from the textile mill. They had a simple eulogy a few weeks later at the playgrounds, the last place where Billy was seen. They placed a small marker in his memory. As they left the playground, they turned for one last tearful glance at the marker's location. Their tears were replaced by fear and wonder. A small boy fitting Billy's description was kneeling at the marker and appeared to be weeping. One onlooker ran toward the figure, hollering, "Billy, Billy." The next moment, the onlooker stopped in his tracks. The small figure turned and spoke, weeping, "I want to go home." Then the boy simply vanished. The textile mill workers in the neighborhood knew this little boy was no longer in this world but the world of the supernatural.

His ghost appeared at playgrounds throughout the neighborhood. Several times throughout the rest of the year, the spirit of Billy was seen and experienced at his current school, Granville Graded School. He was witnessed at the playground at the school by fellow students during games of baseball, playing on the swings and slides and other play equipment.

During lunchtime at school, the teacher often took the students outside on field trips to eat picnic style. Once, two boys and two girls were eating in a circle on the ground under what some called the boys' climbing tree. They heard someone calling their names and realized the frightening calls were coming from the branches of the tree. The ghost boy was sitting in the tree and seemed to be looking at the children with these words on his lips, "I want to go home. I am hungry." Then he vanished.

The years passed, and the boy was seen less and less. The playground of Old West Salem School was developed, and homes were built along Laurel Street between Academy Street and West Street. The location of the school itself was replaced by later homes on Mulberry Street and Academy Street. As I researched my pictorial book of historic West Salem, I interviewed a few older individuals who had attended Granville School in the 1920s. They vaguely remembered a ghost or two associated with the school, and after several older ladies moved into the apartments built on the Granville School site, a sighting occurred. One older lady, who has since passed, moved into the Granville Place Senior Living Apartments on the site of the Old Granville School. She said at the interview in 2002, while her and her friends were served lunch together, the group decided to take a stroll along the fenced-in grounds of a green space developed for them at Academy Street. She noticed a small boy walking along the top of the original rock wall of the old school along Academy Street. The lady became scared and ventured over to the fence to warn the young one that he could get hurt and fall. As she approached, she called to the little boy, who appeared to be humming and playing along the wall to get down. He glanced at her with the most beautiful smile she had ever seen and said, "I am fine, ma'am. I am going home." He turned and proceeded on his way. The humming had become whistling. She watched a few more feet, and he seemed to vanish. She thought at first he may have fallen. The group and the woman went outside the fence where the sidewalk was, but nothing was there. Then, it dawned on the lady, this was the poor little lost boy of her youth. With that, the title of this story was coined.

Chapter 23

Granville School Mystery

The tale of the central character of our story, the Granville Graded School, follows a long line of education establishments in Old West Salem. The mystery of this story paralleled the supernatural events of the lost boy's story, but this tale looks deeper into the school and its personal touch with death.

The Granville Graded School was the fifth public school of Old West Salem. At its opening circa 1913, the school was designated the best and most advanced graded school in the state by the state superintendent of schools. Academically, it lived up to its designation by the state and city leaders. What allowed the school to achieve this designation was developed from a long background of academic excellent in the history of education facilities in Old West Salem. The roots of education were traced back to the first patriarch of West Salem, Brother Gottlieb Schober, also the hero of our first tale. Brother Schober had many accomplishments in the town of Salem, but his crowning one was created by his progressive nature. His love of mankind and his love of children propelled his main interest of championing early schools for all citizens at a time when education was reserved for the rich and privileged. He believed and practiced equality in life and education for all children of God. His Sunday schools were the forerunners of the free schoolhouses that dotted the landscape of the South in the 1830s and 1840s, and he brought them to all the people of Salem. Many Sunday schools were taught at the Krueser farm (circa 1816) in Old West Salem, located on the Old Shallowford Road (circa 1765). The current location of the Krueser farm is the 400 block of South Broad Street. This was the first location of the Old West Salem school.

The second school was built as part of the free schoolhouse programs in 1820. Education became a major need with the arrival of the Industrial Revolution to our country. The federal government, along with the government of the state, followed the lead of Brother Schober and his Sunday schools. Separation of church and state did not get in the way of an alliance brought by Brother Schober to the education forefront. Education for all was available in our state. The Salem Cotton Mill (circa 1830) had petitioned for a free schoolhouse under this program in 1840 because of the array of workers at the mill. In 1847, the school was opened in Old West Salem. It was just north of the mill and in today's landscape would be found at the corner of Liberty and West First Streets. The school existed until the Civil War, when most of the free schoolhouses closed for the duration of the year. The third school of West Salem was held at the Elm Street Chapel beginning in 1867. This was a combination Moravian chapel, Sunday school and public school. The chapel was home to the children until the Old West Salem Graded School was constructed in 1895 on Mulberry Street. Mr. Calvin Wiley, superintendent for the state, headed up the Graded School System in the 1880s. The first graded school was Winston Graded School on West Fourth Street (circa 1882) in Old West End. The Old West Salem Graded School had become obsolete and overcrowded by 1910. The fourth school that contained the tale of our story, Granville Graded School. arrived in 1913.

Mr. Bryant Lee was a neighbor of mine who contributed greatly to the tale of the Granville Graded School. Bryant's father was Charles S. Lee, a builder who had arrived to Old West Salem in 1910 by way of his ancestral home in the state of Virginia. He was brought down with a prominent architect, designer and other builders from Virginia to construct the estate of Richard J. and Katherine Reynolds named Reynolda. He and his company constructed the road system into Reynolda, which became the Reynolda Road of today. During the 1910s, his company employed more than one hundred workers. This made his company one of the top employers of Winston-Salem. In 1916, he secured the contract to build the modern road system in Winston-Salem from Mr. R.J. Reynolds, the tobacco magnate and patriarch of the town. He also constructed the sidewalks that still today are recognized by builders and historians alike for their superior quality compared with those done later. In fact, his initials, C.S. Lee, can still be seen imprinted on the old sidewalks throughout the city. He was a lifelong resident of West Salem, and his house at 224 South Green Street is still standing. Mr. Lee built the Grandville Graded School and the massive granite wall that surrounds the school as well. The school has been razed, but the wall stands in testimony to Mr. Lee's artisanship. Even to this day, builders and stone workers come to the city to admire his work at the school and at the Reynolda estate.

Bryant Lee, his son, related the story of an early student and the fate that befell him at the Granville Graded School. C.S Lee cried when he told the story to Bryant, praying that the same fate would not befall him. Bryant related:

> *My dad told me this story to make me aware always of my surroundings, because evil could be around every corner. My dad had warned me several times before of the dangers of the swimming pool. The Granville Graded School was one of the first public schools that contained a swimming pool in the basement. My dad did not like the plans of a large body of water brought to a place surrounded by children. In fact, before he began building the school, he had warned the school system of the nightmare that could come from a pool so close to these children. I tried to reassure him. I said,*

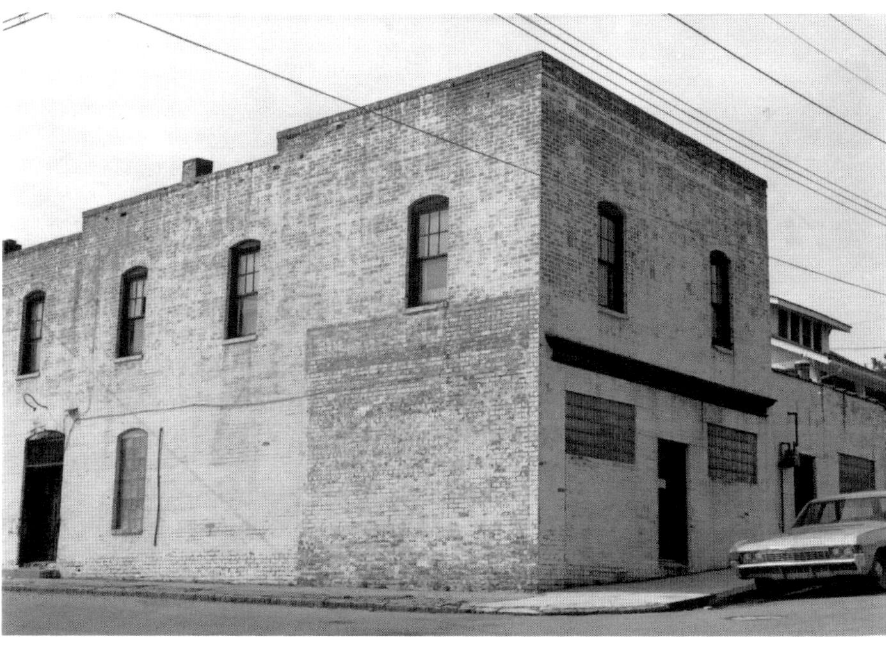

The building at Wachovia Street and South Poplar Street had many incarnations, including grocery stores, a textile mill and an instructional building for Piedmont Bible College.

> *"Dad, everyone knows the pool to us is just the neighborhood bathtub." Dad looked at me very sternly and relayed an incident that very few knew of the school and the pool.*

Bryant hesitated, and with a change of disposition, he related this part of the story:

> *The textile workers lived throughout West Salem. The ones who lived on Wachovia Street, Apple Street, Albert Street westward through Wachovia Highlands to the present Peters Creek Parkway were a motley crew. Many of the children of the textile workers were of low income. Most were embarrassed when they went to school since their clothes were often threadbare and they had mostly hand-me-down shoes. Some had no shoes, even in winter. Even I attended a birthday party of one of my school friends at Granville in the late 1920s. I felt so sorry for the small log cabin that the people lived in. The floors were dirt, and the mother seemed to always have to sweep out the house when I came over. I realized after talking to my dad the floors were not dirt, but rock from the old quarries of the Paper Mill Settlement of the eighteenth century.*

The log cabins with stone floors were prevalent in the mill settlement during the time period of 1830–40. Today's siding and modernization covers the more than two-hundred-year-old history of these structures. Bryant continued, "Children can be very cruel sometimes. They would often chastise the mill students since the clothes they wore were full of holes, as were their shoes, and those who often came to school barefooted were referred to as barefeets." One of the barefooted grade students from the mill family became a victim of a cruel joke gone terribly wrong.

Several students stayed after school on a Friday to complete some work due to absences. A late-spring cold had sickened many in the school. These students were some of the last students to become sick, and they were here to make up their work. One of the students was a barefoot kid, as the other children called him. The school would have been abandoned for the weekend since all of the faculty and teachers had already gone. The kids somehow found their way to the basement, the "bathtub" of their neighborhood. The pool was dark and scary. They kidded the barefoot kid and told him the pool had an alligator in it and it was hungry. The poor kid believed them and tried to escape the pool area. He panicked, tripped and fell into the stagnant murky water of the unclean pool. The pool had been closed due to the cold

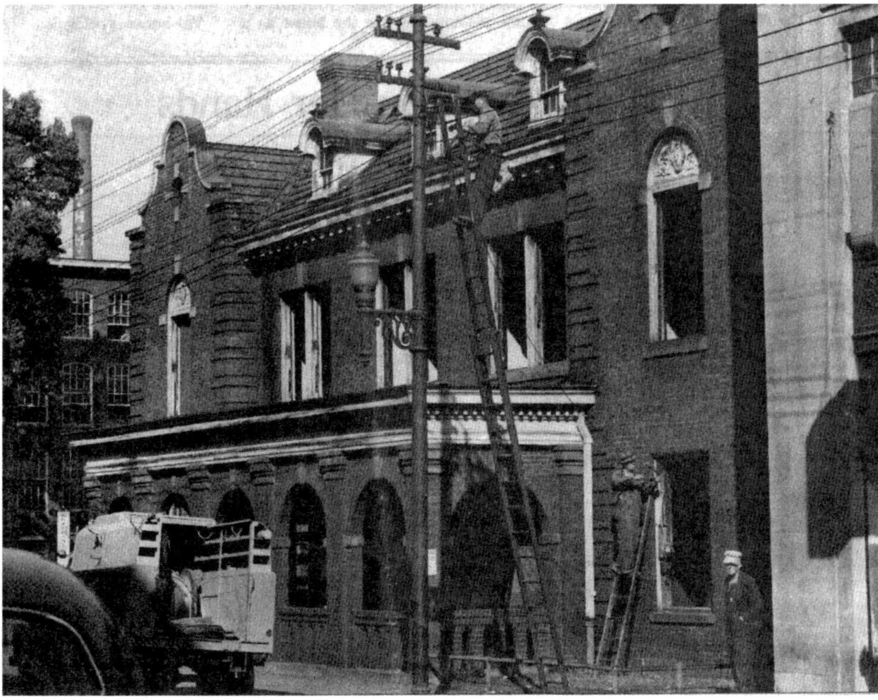

The Old Forsyth County Jail (circa 1870s) on Main Street at Fifth Street downtown Old Winston.

outbreak and had not been cleaned in a while. The other kids panicked as well. They called to the child in the water, but the barefoot boy had seemed to have sunk like a rock.

Bryant said, "The young boy was gone. The incident scared the children, and they ran. My dad said the children told their parents, but the investigation of the missing boy took a mysterious turn. The police were called in to check the depths of the pool, but no evidence of the boy was found. The investigation turned into a missing person report. The parents were devastated by the events." Bryant had explained that his father had heard of this mystery of the Granville pool through the city workers he corresponded with while securing building permits. The school and the pool, which he had never wanted to build, had taken a life. Bryant told his dad maybe the child had not drowned; someone may have saved him, and that was that. Though his father assured him the boy had gone to heaven, Bryant found out much later the barefoot boy was probably dead, but the missing body has stayed a mystery to this day.

Bryant believed the boy's death was confirmed when the poltergeist action began in the neighborhood not long after his passing. The kids in the neighborhood had Saturday excursions to several key spots in the neighborhood. Even the mill kids were invited to attend. The A&P food store (circa 1918), at South Green and First Streets, was visited by many families. A penny cookie was always a treat there. If not to the chain grocery stores, which began to arrive to Winston-Salem and eventually squeezed out the mom-and-pop grocery stores, their shopping trips took them to the Tesh's grocery store, next to the A&P on Green Street, or Barney's Food Store, five blocks south on Green Street.

In the 1920s and 1930s, there was a grocery store on every corner in West Salem. Seven grocery stores were along South Green Street alone. The scary part about these grocery stores was the visits by the barefoot boy, who enjoyed playing tricks throughout the store. His barefoot spirit was often seen appearing around corners and in the shadows.

Even creepy things occurred at the local barbershop, where all the kids would have their hair cut. Chitty's Barber Shop was at South Green and Wachovia Streets. Several kids reported seeing the barefoot boy around the barbershop, and sometimes he was even seen in some of the barber chairs. Mr. Chitty even swore to the children he had cut the little fellow's hair just a couple days before the sightings.

"The hot dog house," as Bryant called it, was also the scene of a sighting of the ghost. The building still exists as property of Piedmont International University at the corner of South Green and Apple Streets.

All of these establishments are now history, but who knows when the barefoot boy will reappear. The supernatural events that permeate the West Salem, Old Salem and Old Winston landscape are a reminder that when something becomes history, it does not mean it will never come back.

Chapter 24

The White-Haired Man

This tale was relayed by an old family friend who had the unfortunate opportunity to share his residence with a terrifying entity that could not pass on. Those who experienced its company were not the better for it. The man and wife moved into the nineteenth-century rambling Victorian wood-framed structure. It was three stories, and in the early 1950s, it had seen its better days. The location was South Marshall Street between West Street and Tanners Lane. South Marshall Street was a dividing line between East Salem and West Salem. The first industrial area of the Salem Moravians in the area was located one block to the north of our tale, circa 1769. Homes were built along with the industrial buildings as early as 1800 and onward to the 1850s. The structure in which the couple resided was one of these old homeplaces.

The 1940s and 1950s saw a change developing in Salem, East and West. The Great Depression and World War II had not allowed the citizens to maintain or update their properties. The tightness of the economy during the Depression and war years made life during this fifteen-year time period very frugal. Also, during the 1940s and 1950s, the area saw the development of the modern suburbs that grew immensely throughout the second half of the twentieth century. The older neighborhoods experienced a one-two punch from the Depression and war, and the exodus of the families into the suburbs increased that negativity. The older homes along Marshall Street had seen their better days, and the paranormal activity in the home of the couple made their lives even worse.

Industry existed alongside the couple's home. Within the two blocks of the couple's home was an old cigar factory (circa 1890), the Greyhound bus

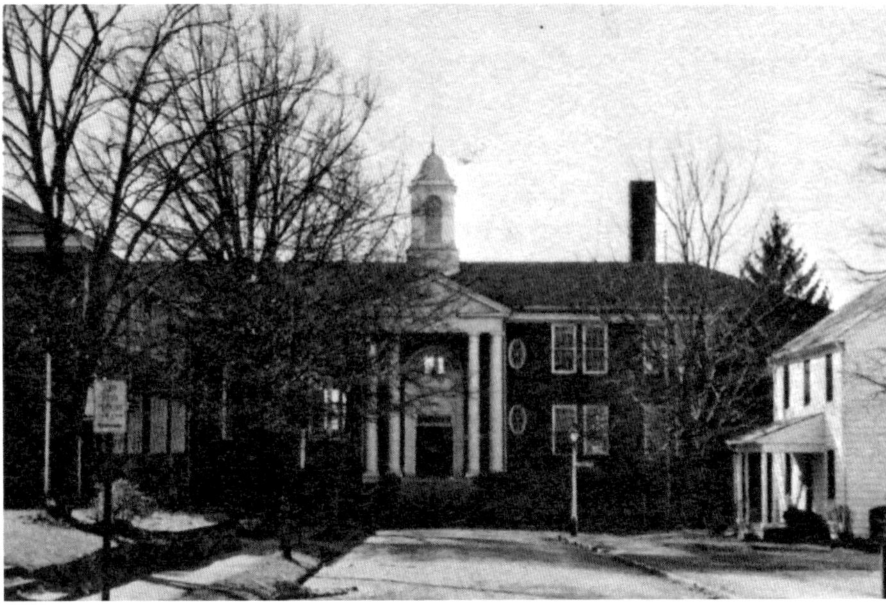

Old Central School on Church Street (circa 1920s) was built on land that was part of the African American graveyard of St. Phillips Church (circa 1822).

terminal (circa 1930), the Coca-Cola Bottling Plant (circa 1920s) and a metal fabricating business (circa 1940s). The Southbound Railway (circa 1910) ran behind the older homes of Marshall Street. Even a mineral springs resort had existed for a short time within the block. The Southbound Railway and the mineral springs resort became the catalyst that created a horror that plagued this quiet mix of home and businesses from the 1920s to 1950s.

Before the Southbound Railway arrived to West Salem in 1910, a different type of business found its way to West Salem. The Mystic Springs (circa 1898) were built on the future site of the Stratford Metal Fabricating Company of the 1940s. The metal fabricating company was razed in 2012, and the site now serves as overflow parking for the Old Salem Center. The Mystic Springs also produced a bottled water advertised as an elixir that could cure many ailments of the time. An advertisement dated 1899 appeared in the *Winston-Salem Journal*. It read:

> *The Mystic Springs Water—Nature's Great Panacea: A positive cure for indigestion and all forms of liver, kidney and bladder troubles endorsed by some of Winston's most prominent physicians and some of our most distinguished world citizens. Its affect upon the system is the most soothing and healing of*

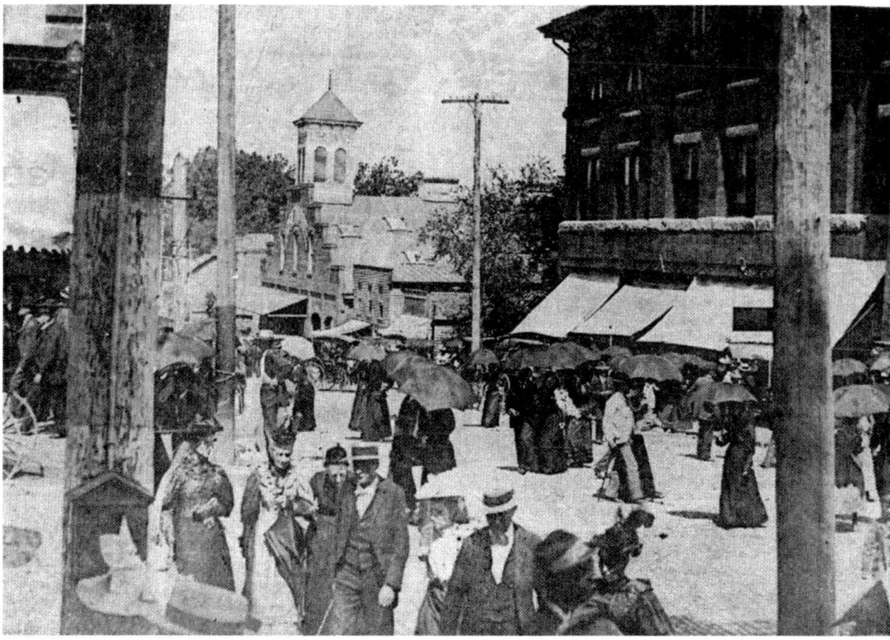

The Browns' warehouse (circa 1870s) was home to tobacco auctions, county fairs and entertainment, including minstrel shows and circuses.

> *any of the mineral waters now advertised at high prices. A trial will convince the most skeptical of its great value as a remedy agent. Arrangements for furnishing sample bottles free on physician's recommendation will be made at once. Address the Mystic Springs Water Company, Winston, North Carolina.*

The Mystic Springs and the Mystic Springs Water Company was greeted with open arms by the city because of the enticement of the mineral springs, whose promise dates back to 1850 in Piedmont, North Carolina. The Sauratown Mountains, including Hanging Rock and Pilot Mountain, were home to one of the first mineral springs, the Piedmont Springs, in 1849. The Piedmont Springs had the rolling hills and brooks of the mountains. The large Piedmont Springs Hotel was built to accommodate the crowds who gathered for leisure and relaxation, as well as the medicinal waters. The mineral springs were connected to an elaborate swimming pool. The architecture of the pool and spa were similar to the baths of ancient Rome. Many of the wealthy and well-to-do families traveled to the Piedmont Spring and Resort Hotel from Winston and Salem, North Carolina. In Winston, North Carolina in 1898, the Piedmont Spring Resort became the mentor for Mystic Springs.

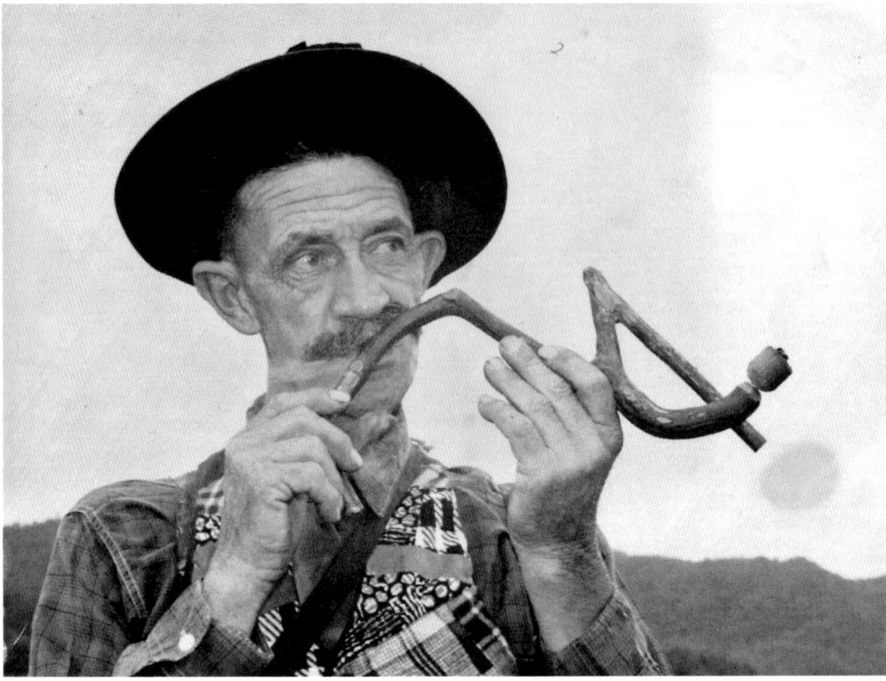

This old gentleman was showing off the array of smoking devises to be used with tobacco. The white-haired man of our tale saw these old devices in his nightmares.

A smaller version, of course, without the hotel was present. The Mystic Springs complex tapped Tanners Run Creek with a connection that ran along the natural rolling hill from Marshall Street down to the creek. In today's landscape, the creek runs parallel to the Old Salem walkway. The walkway was the original location of the Southbound train tracks that followed its path into Winston-Salem. An understanding of the location of the mineral springs and the Southbound Railroad will our readers a picture in their mind as to help them visualize what comes next.

The couple of our story knew nothing of the mineral springs and the sordid connections with the railway when they moved into the home into Marshall Street. Their lives may have been much improved if they had. From the get-go, the husband felt there was something wrong in the house. He did not like the overwhelming feeling of dread he experienced every time he entered the house. His wife felt completely different. She said she had always wanted to live in a nice, big old house in Salem, and her husband would just have to deal with it.

They had lived in the house about a week when the husband reported to his wife the nightmares he had been experiencing since they moved in. She was skeptical since he had not wanted to move in the house. After having the same dreams over and over again, her husband thought something was going to happen to them. The husband told the bizarre nightmare to his wife:

> *I was coming home, and it was almost dark. I was on Marshall Street, passing the intersection of West Street. As I approached the Stratford Metal Company, I literally dropped my teeth. The company had disappeared and in its place was an exquisite walkway to what looked like marble columns. The entrance followed a beautiful path almost like gold. Over the entrance was an arc, a Roman arc, I suppose. A large marquee was attached to the top of the arc with a drawing of a large eye. It said Mystic Springs, but I could not make out the complete name. I stopped for a moment and peered down into the darkness. A pale light seemed to be coming from bonfires from below. That is when I saw the woman of my dream.*

The wife had to stop her husband with that statement. She replied rather loudly, "I am the woman of your dreams!"

He continued, "No, the woman who keeps appearing in all my dreams. She beckons me to come with her. She is dressed in what I believe to be Egyptian garments. I walk closer to get a better look at this situation, and I notice the path turns into four flights of granite staircases extending down into, I believe, water."

The man stopped, sweating profusely and shaking uncontrollably. The wife told her husband to calm down, but he explained that he had such a feeling of dread and despair after having this dream that, even in his waking state, it scared the life out of him. The wife told him the dream meant nothing or, if it did, probably it is something he is putting off or something he should finish. The wife's recommendation was if he had the dream again, to go with the imaginary woman and see where the stairs led. She believed if he did this, the nightmares would go away.

The man trusted his wife totally and was determined to get to the bottom of it. The next night before retiring to their bedroom, the wife assured the man everything would be okay.

The next day, the woman asked over breakfast if the nightmare had come back. A definite yes, he replied with a strange look on his face. He asked his wife once more, "Can we move, please?" She was beginning to question her husband's sanity. But he story he told was very frightening and macabre:

> *The dream played out exactly the same. As I walked toward the woman, she appeared to walk—no, glide backwards down the flight of stairs.*

> *As I trailed after her, keeping my distance, I began to hear voices I had never heard before. The bonfire and marble columns with Egyptian-style hieroglyphic writing on them seemed to come alive with movement. By this time, the woman had entered the water, and a pool surrounded her to the waist. She beckoned me to join. I noticed several other Egyptian figures in the water around her. As I drew closer to the pool, the surroundings seem to become brighter. I was still outdoors, and it was pitch black in the sky. As I left the gaze of the sky, I returned to the lady and her comrades. I was frozen with fear. The Egyptian lady and those around her had turned into grotesque demons, devils like I could have never imagined. The woman and the others began to approach me and they wanted me to join them forever. I do not know how, but I managed to turn and go up the steps. My speed increased, but I could hear and feel their presence behind me. As I climbed the steps and made my way down the path, I turned when I had made it to the sidewalk. To my astonishment, the Mystic Eye, columns and all else had vanished. The dark Stratford Metal building stood alone.*

That day and for several thereafter, the man was still worried. He began to see things out of the corner of his eyes and the reflection of the Egyptian woman in mirrors, and he heard voices, moaning and groaning late at night in the house. He believed he had gone crazy. His wife took him to the doctor, who reassured him and his wife that he was fit as a fiddle. The husband's dreams and nightmares were just a figment of his imagination. The doctor recommended they take a vacation, so they took a weekend off with a trip to Greensboro, North Carolina.

Once they returned back to Marshall Street, the couple put the nonsense behind them. Before the man went to bed after reading the local paper, suddenly they heard a heavy thump upstairs. The man went to see what had happened. The woman jumped when she heard a man scream, and she hollered for her husband. As she began to climb the stairs, she heard someone walking toward her. She met her husband at the top of the stairs and almost fainted. Her pitiful husband was standing there with a terrified look on his face. He had been so scared that the hair on his head had turned a snowy white. In a mirror, the white-haired man had found the Egyptian woman, who had returned to collect the man to share her Mystic Spring with him. He had broken the mirror and fled. He and his wife left the home and never returned, leaving everything behind. The couple had no more problems after leaving the house. After the couple left the home, the block of houses was razed. No one in the neighborhood knows if any problem continued, but the white-haired man would always remember his experience.

Chapter 25

The Haunted Grocery Store

Our final tale could hold the answer to many of the questions of the supernatural experiences that have been profiled in our journey of the unknown. The sequences of activities that occurred in our story led to a horrific act of terror for those involved and, even worse, for those who may be involved in the future of our town. The spirits, ghosts, haints and even the devil himself could be connected to the evil in our haunted grocery store.

The tale unfolds with the history of grocery stores not much different from this one. Mom-and-pop grocery stores have been a fixture in Winston and Salem throughout the twentieth century, when there was literally a grocery store on every corner. Winston-Salem in 1917 was chosen as a port of entry because of the national and international shipping ventures of the Reynolds and Hanes empires. Our port of entry was also the farthest inland port in the world. This may have helped to create more than 150 mom-and-pop grocery stores in Winston-Salem in 1917. This is amazing when you realize the downtown city limits was a mere three- to four-mile radius. Mom-and-pop grocery stores served many functions other than just providing grocery merchandise. Each community in Winston and Salem was made up of a few streets. The grocery store was the meeting place for neighbors and the place for the local adults to share news and to shop, and some even had the proverbial checkerboard. The chain grocery stores arrived to the city in 1918 after World War I. The Piggly Wiggly was the first, followed by the A&P, the Atlantic and Pacific Tea Company. The mom-and-pop stores competed with the chain stores for more than thirty years. The 1950s brought the suburbs

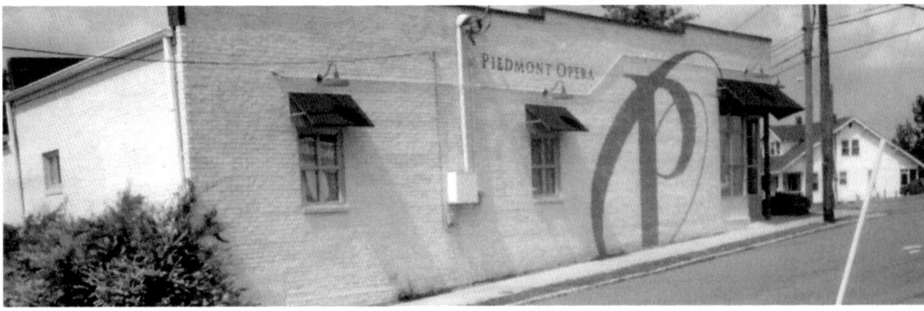

The old A&P grocery store (circa 1919) at the corner of Green and West First Streets.

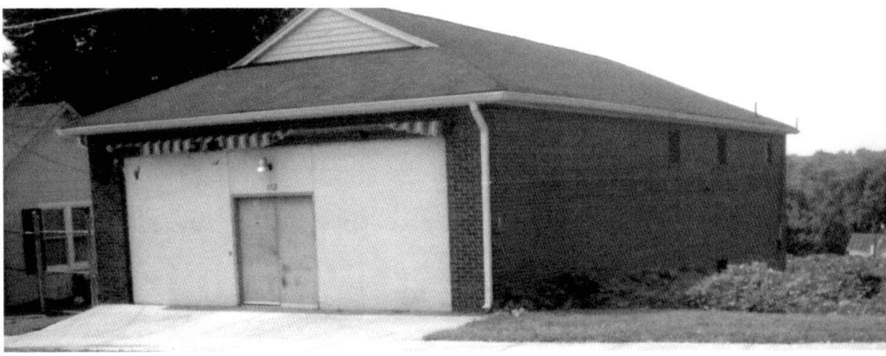

The Tesh grocery store and meat market (circa 1919), where the killing of the old meat cutter took place.

and the shopping centers. The local grocery stores were able to hang on in several of the older neighborhoods. The Green Front Cash Store, the place of my youth and the old-timers, lasted the longest.

Tesh's Grocery and Meat Market at 103 South Green Street was a local mom-and-pop store that lasted until 1973. Mrs. Tesh had no intentions of closing or retiring. She had run the store for more than fifty-five years with her husband, who had passed a few years before. Mrs. Tesh's customer base existed in West Salem and West End. Her business even extended into Buena Vista and other wealthy neighborhoods across the city. Her meat market was one of the main things that set her apart from all the other mom-and-pop grocery stores. Mr. Snow, her meat cutter, had thirty years of experience practicing his craft. Many times over the years, his skills had been scouted by rival stores, as well as chain stores, but neither Mrs. Tesh nor her meat cutter had any intentions discontinuing the services they had performed so well over the years.

I am sure my readers by now know happy endings are few and far between in my tales. The evil that always seems to raise its head from below the earth or above it, I believe, arrived at Tesh's Grocery Store's back door on a cold dark night in 1973. Mrs. Tesh was closing up, and she asked Mr. Snow if he was ready to leave. He reported that he planned to stay late and prepare the meat orders for Friday's delivery, which was usually the busiest of the week, and sleep on the cot in the back room. This was not unusual for Mr. Snow because of his work ethic. Mrs. Tesh wished him good night and said she would see him in the morning. That Friday night was the last time anyone would see Mr. Snow alive.

No one truly knows what transpired that eventful night. The police attributed it to alcohol and bad luck. Until her dying day, Mrs. Tesh believed something came for Mr. Snow, something evil. Old Scratch himself had been after Mr. Snow, or so Mr. Snow often told his friends. Mrs. Tesh gave the report to the police:

> *I arrived about 6:00 a.m. on Friday morning. I noticed the lights were all off, which was a little odd since Mr. Snow was usually working by now. As I entered the side door, I heard a noise—strange. I could plainly hear the saw of the meat cutter running. I called for Mr. Snow, but no response. "Mr. Snow, you cannot cut the meat in the dark," I said, and I turned the corner to enter the back room when I nearly fainted. I know I blacked out for a minute or two. I have seen terrible accidents in the kitchen and butcher shop over my many years in the grocery business. This was the most heinous and gruesome scene I have ever witnessed. Mr. Snow was draped across the meat counter, the saw was at his throat still running, blood everywhere and his poor head laid on the floor below the saw.*

Mrs. Tesh never returned to the store again. Her family was sent to clean it out and sell what they could. The doors were padlocked. Lights were turned off by Duke Power, the electric company. The police investigation said Mr. Snow had suffered a self-inflicted wound to the neck, prompted by alcohol abuse. No further investigation was done. Mrs. Tesh had a good business head on her shoulders. She always believed there was more to the investigation than what was told.

The back door of the shop was unlocked. She had locked the store herself, and Mr. Snow never went out the back door. The meat cutter's saw had an automatic shut off. If you did not have your hand physically on the handle and push the meat through the saw, it would shut off. Mr. Snow was beheaded. Even if he had wanted to commit suicide, this would not be the way to do it. He would have needed help to accomplish this suicide. No other person was found to be involved—but what if it was not a person? Mrs. Tesh often said Mr. Snow had his demons.

The evil that struck that night was not about to go away, even after the terrible tragedy of the meat cutter. The old structure stayed empty for several years. The family would not go back into the store again, nor could Mrs. Tesh let go of the establishment or sell it. Only after Mrs. Tesh's passing did the family try to sell it. Within weeks after the accident, the neighbors next door to the building, the Hawns, reported strange lights and noises coming from it. They called the police on several occasions to investigate whether someone had broken in, but each time the police found nothing. Mrs. Tesh's family had given the Hawns a key to the place because they could not bear to return to the establishment.

The family on the other side of the store had the same problems, except their encounters with the terrors, as they called the evil, were also physical. Their children enjoyed playing in the backyard on play equipment. They had begun to complain that the monster was scaring them. At first, the parents thought the children were making it up or just imaging it. Then a few days later, the children ran into the house sobbing uncontrollably. Once the mother calmed the children down, the story they relayed changed everything for the family. The children said, "We were not bothering the monster in the old building. It came out of the building and said things we do not understand. We are not going back outside to play anymore, Mommy." The mother went to the building and began to scream for whatever it was that was in the building needed to stop messing with her children. She called her husband at work, and he called the police. The police arrived and were given the story. The police went to the other side of the Hawns and got the key to the old store. This had seemed to become a regular occurrence. Again, nothing was found. No one was in the store. The police were puzzled since the man or monster who supposedly was there was not. The entity was large, but the description did not fit the dead man of Mr. Snow in anyway.

The family had had enough with the problems at the building and moved away shortly thereafter. The empty house began to exhibit strange lights, moaning sounds were heard and neighbors even reported seeing the house shake uncontrollably as if an earthquake had occurred. That house was the only one affected. The police were called to the block once more and were surprised that the problem was not with the old building but with the house next door. They investigated and again found nothing. When they heard the story of the shaking house, they investigated the exterior of the place. The police became confused because cracks were found along the base of the home, along with several broken panes of glass in the windows. An inspector was called out to the house to check the foundation. The foundation had been compromised, and the house was condemned. The house was razed a month later.

On the opposite side of the store, the Hawns continued to have problems with the old store. They swore one late night the noise was so great and the lights that emitted from the store were almost blinding. Enough was enough for them, and they moved shortly thereafter. The Hawns' old homestead and the old store remained empty for several years. In 1977, the store building was finally bought by a cooperative group, which was going to reopen it as a co-op food store. In the late 1970s, the movement of natural foods and communal businesses became popular during the administration of President Jimmy Carter. The co-op store was very successful early on and was received well by the community. No strange things occurred at first. After about a year, the workers reported strange movements throughout the store. The items on the shelf began to move and were often found out of place. The back room of the old meat cutter was not used and was closed off. Sounds were often heard in that room when no one was back there. They even reported hearing a motor or a machine-type noise. One worker identified the noise as that of a saw, but nothing was found. The workers began to be too scared to be in the store alone. Always two or more workers were to be there at all times. It appeared the evil had returned.

The co-op business had enough, and the store moved. The building had been empty for at least a year when it was bought by a construction company, which used the building only as storage. I had the opportunity to speak to the owners of the construction company. They had heard some of the stories from the locals but did not think much of it. One evening as the workers worked late, they began to hear things throughout the store. They even experienced strange lights, even though most of the lighting had been disconnected. The company owner said, "We use the building only for storage. I tell my men to be finished before dark."

The building was used by the construction company until it was sold by the BB&T developers for the new semipro baseball field that was coming to the area. The old store that sat on the hill was the last structure to be razed as the building of the ball field proceeded. Could the evil that had been involved with this building and many building and structures throughout Winston-Salem have just disappeared? Only time will tell if the evil of the haunted grocery store will return. As construction and modernization continues in and around the old crossroads and Old West Salem, the evil hopefully will be history.

BIBLIOGRAPHY

Bradley, Betsy Hunter. *The Works: The Industrial Architecture of the United States.* Cambridge, UK: Oxford University Press, 1999.

Bricker, Michael. *Historic Forsyth County*. Charleston, SC: Arcadia Publishing, 2013.

———. *Historic West Salem*. Charleston, SC: Arcadia Publishing, 2006.

———. *Winston-Salem: A Twin City History*. Charleston, SC: The History Press, 2008.

———. *Winston-Salem Through Time*. London: Fonthill Media, 2014.

———. *Ye Olde West Salem Scrapbook*. Winston-Salem, NC: West Salem Historical Association, 2005.

Brownlee, Fambrough. *Winston-Salem: A Pictorial History*. Norfolk, VA: Donning Company, 1977.

Church, William Hal. Interview by Michael Bricker, November 2002.

Cranford, Reverend William A. *Christ Moravian Church: The First One-Hundred Years*. Winston-Salem, NC: Centennial Committee, 1997.

Davis, Chester. "Voglar Service: 1858—A Century of Service in the Mortuary Field." *Winston-Salem Journal*, October 16, 1963.

Forsyth County Historic Properties Commission, Information Forms.

Fries, Adelaide L. *Forsyth: A County on the March*. Chapel Hill: University of North Carolina Press, 1976.

Fries, Adelaide L., ed., et al. *Records of the Moravians in NorCambridgeth Carolina*. Vols. 1–11. Raleigh: North Carolina Historical Commission and State Department of Archives and History, 1949.

Hartley, Michael, and Martha Boxley. "Salem Survey." Raleigh: North Carolina Division of Archives and History, 1997.

Lee, Bryant W. Interview by Michael Bricker, March 2003.

National Register of Historic Places, Study Guides of Local Historic Districts: Ardmore, Downtown North, Holly Avenue, Washington Park, West End, West Salem.

North Carolina Historical Review. January 1924–82. Published by the North Carolina Historical Commission, Raleigh, NC.

Peoples Press, 1830–70. Salem, NC.

Rondthaler, Reverend Edward. *The Memorabilia of Fifty Years, 1887–1927*. Raleigh, NC: Edwards and Broughton Company, 1928.

Ruger & Stoner. Bird's Eye View of Winston-Salem. 1891.

Sanborn Insurance Company. Map series: 1885, 1890, 1895, 1900, 1907, 1912, 1917, 1949.

Smith, James Howell. "Industry and Commerce 1896–1975." *Winston-Salem in History*. Vol. 8. Winston-Salem, NC: Historic Winston, 1977.

Taylor, Gwynne Stephens. *From Frontier to Factory*. North Carolina Department of Cultural Resources, Division of Archives and History, and Winston-Salem/Forsyth County Historic Properties Commission, City-County Planning Board of Forsyth County and Winston-Salem. Winston-Salem, 1981.

Tise, Larry Edward. "The Churches." *Winston-Salem in History*. Vol. 10. Winston-Salem, NC: Historic Winston, 1976.

———. "Industry and Commerce 1766–1896." *Winston-Salem in History*. Vol. 7. Winston-Salem, NC: Historic Winston, 1977.

Tursi, Frank. *Winston-Salem: A History*. Winston-Salem, NC: John F. Blair, 1994.

Vogler, E.A. Map of Winston and Salem. 1876, revised 1884.

Wellman, Manley Wade. "Transportation and Communication." *Winston-Salem in History*. Vol. 4. Winston-Salem, NC: Historic Winston, 1977.

Winston-Salem City Directories, 1880–1950. North Carolina Room, Forsyth County Library.

Winston-Salem Journal and Sentinel, 1870–1950. North Carolina Room, Forsyth County Library microfiche library section.

Winston-Salem Journal and Sentinel, 1960–2007. Author's personal collection.

Woodard, Sarah. "Report on the History of Five Bridges in Salem." Old Salem, Inc., 1996.

Also cited are interviews by author, 1960–1965, with Mr. William Johns and old-timers all born in the late nineteenth century; Mr. Frank Jones and Mr. Roy Thompson, employees of *Winston-Salem Journal and Sentinel*; Mr. Robert Turner, proprietor of the Green Front Cash Store; and Mr. John Levin Brietz and family.

About the Author

As a sixty-plus-year resident of Winston-Salem, author Michael L. Bricker has combed the older neighborhoods of Old Salem and Old Winston in search of local history. He is the lay historian of Old West Salem and founder of the West Salem Historical Association. He presided over the nomination of West Salem as a historic neighborhood on the National Register of Historic Places and the Preserve America nomination for the West Salem Historic District as well. Through the Preserve America nomination, Historic West Salem became only the nineteenth Preserve America Neighborhood in the United States. Preceding this publication, he has authored five local history books on West Salem, Winston-Salem and Forsyth County.